Overcome Anxiety:

A Self Help Toolkit for Anxiety Relief and Panic Attacks

Matthew Lewis, PHD

www.DrMattLewis.com

ISBN-10: 1536842753
ISBN-13: 978-1536842753

DEDICATION

This book is dedicated to all of the former students who have passed through my doors to seek guidance, help, and understanding. It would not have been possible without your vulnerability and honesty.

Table of Contents

Introduction.. 1

How to Use This Book... 5

Before You Start: The Importance of Mindset................... 9

Theory

The Road to Anxiety

Chapter 1: The Components of Anxiety........................... 21

Chapter 2: Our Troublesome Brains.............................. 25

Chapter 3: The Pathways to Anxiety............................. 32

Chapter 4: Anxiety Disorders.................................... 46

Practical Exercises

Step 1: Calming the Mind

Chapter 5: Getting to Know Yourself............................ 53

Chapter 6: Calming the Mind.................................... 65

Step 2: Dealing with Anxious Thoughts and Feelings

Chapter 7: Defusion: Managing Anxious Thoughts............... 81

Chapter 8: Expansion: Managing Anxious Feelings.............. 89

Chapter 9: Engagement... 93

Step 3: Taking Action

Chapter 10: Overcoming Fear....................................... 99

Chapter 11: How to be Confident at Doing Anything............ 105

Chapter 12: The Fear Project.. 115

Emergency Exercises: Managing Fight, Flight, or Freeze

Chapter 13: Calming the Anxiety Response....................... 123

Chapter 14: Panic Attacks... 134

Moving Forward

Chapter 15: What Next?... 147

Chapter 16: Powerful Essentials................................... 159

Finally.. 174

Further Details and Resources...................................... 175

About the Author... 176

Notes... 177

Introduction

On a warm afternoon towards the end of Spring in 2014, I was sitting in my university office when there was a knock on my door. I looked through the glass to see a student I recognised from one of my health psychology classes. I smiled, gestured for her to come in and swivelled my chair around to meet her gaze, but I couldn't, because her eyes were firmly fixed on the floor.

Without looking up, she reached out her hand and gave me an envelope that was addressed to me. I tore it open and pulled out a four page handwritten letter. It started, 'Dear Matt, I feel unable to speak about how I feel at the moment, so I thought it would be best to put my words into writing and explain it that way..."

The letter went on to describe, in great detail, how anxiety had crippled her life and left her feeling unable to function. She had fallen behind in her academic work, withdrawn from all social activities, wasn't able to sleep more than a few hours each night, and could see no way out. She cried as I read her words and I barely managed to hold back my own tears.

She wasn't the first student to open up to me about her anxiety and she wouldn't be the last. As my academic career developed, I found more and more of my time was being taken up by students seeking me out to talk about their personal anxiety and ask for advice and guidance. I always tried to be open and warm towards students, and I think they often found it easier to talk to someone in my position – someone accessible who taught them about mental health – rather than their parents, friends, university counsellors, or medical professionals. I occupied the middle ground between the 'too personal' and the 'too official'.

Having suffered from severe anxiety, I was able to be empathetic and understood many of their fears and struggles. I could also provide them with the powerful hope that it's possible to change your relationship with anxiety and manage it in a way that not just helps you get by in life, but enables you to thrive, while still living by your core values and being true to yourself. I was able to explain how someone like me, who was scared of speaking on the phone and terrified of social gatherings, was now able to regularly lecture in front of more than 200 students.

I would listen to them carefully, discuss strategies that could help put their coursework back on track, and then suggest they seek help from the university support services or their General Practitioner. Like all people, students found it difficult to find help for their anxiety; often limited to ten minute appointments with their local GP and faced with waiting lists of six months or longer to see a psychologist or psychotherapist. University counsellors helped in the cases that they could, but often also had to refer cases to the local health service.

Over the years, as the trickle of students turned into a steady flow, I started working on a guide to help with everyday anxiety that students could take away with them after their appointments. The guide was designed to be preventative – to stop early symptoms developing into clinical problems – but also to go beyond that; to build confidence, and help them become unstuck and move forward with all the things they needed to do in order to pass the course and get on with their lives.

Eventually, students who didn't suffer from anxiety, but

had heard the exercises were helpful in building more confident and positive lives, started to approach me and ask to have access to the guide. The guide developed into an online course and then into this book.

Although initially developed to help the students I taught, the approach used in the book isn't age or student specific. It includes background information on how anxiety can develop in people of all ages, alongside preventative and interventional exercises derived from a breadth of research on managing anxiety and building confidence.

The approach uses evidenced-based exercises from the areas of mindfulness, Acceptance and Commitment Therapy, and positive psychology. Anxiety can make us feel paralysed, and sometimes the smallest and quickest of tasks can seem insurmountable, so the information has been reduced into small chunks, using brief chapters that can be digested easily and quickly. With a workbook format, it can be used as a toolkit for anxiety relief and provides practical help for calming and reducing panic attacks.

The book starts with some background information explaining why and how anxiety develops and then highlights the evidence that the book's main principles are built on. Although it may be tempting to skip these parts, understanding your anxiety and being convinced by evidence that the exercises really do work should help to bring positive change more quickly, while also increasing your motivation to apply the practices. The theory section is concise, so won't take long to read. However, you can start at the practical exercises if you really want to get started straight away.

There are three main steps in this revolutionary approach and I've seen it change people's lives time and time again. You're going to learn how to:

1. Calm the mind
2. Deal with anxious thoughts and feelings
3. Take action

So the method goes beyond managing anxiety, it will also help you to become unstuck, build confidence and start REALLY living. Using the latest scientific and academic research, you will be able to:

- Understand how and why anxiety develops.
- Develop a mindset that will allow you to see anxiety in a completely different way.
- Create the foundation for a calm and peaceful mind.
- Learn to effectively handle anxious thoughts and feelings as they arise.
- Tame the voice in your head and reduce anxiety without losing your edge.
- Become unstuck and able to take action in situations that you would normally avoid, withdraw, or distract yourself from.
- Begin to take steps to create a fulfilling and meaningful life.

The book contains:

- Step-by-step practical exercises.
- Access to audio exercises and online resources.
- An end of book project to help apply all of the learned skills.

This book will be helpful for those who struggle with:

- Anxiety
- Anxiety Disorder
- Generalized Anxiety
- Social Anxiety
- Panic Attacks
- Panic Disorder
- Agoraphobia
- Health Anxiety

How to Use This Book

This book was written to be read easily and quickly, with the intention that you begin to understand your anxiety and start applying the practical exercises as quickly as possible. So I recommend you read the book in its entirety to begin with, practising the exercises along the way. This should give you a feel of what works best for you. It is worth keeping in mind that it may take time for some of the practices to reveal their full potential, this is why they are called practices. While you will see some immediate positive changes after many of the exercises, others will take a little more time before they reveal their true power.

Many of the exercises don't require huge changes; they are small nudges that will subtly push you in a more peaceful and confident direction, making a positive long-term impact over your life. While you may think it would be best to make huge changes very quickly, you'll find that change is more successful when done at a calm and steady pace. Think tortoise not hare. This book is real, practical, and very effective. Methods that promise instant and magical transformations lose their impact when we have to leave our comfort zone and the fairy dust blows away. The benefits of doing the exercises will steadily build over time. Soon you will start to find your relationship with anxiety changing for the better, along with a growing sense of peace, and the courage to tackle issues and pursue goals that fit your values, helping you to become unstuck and move forward.

FINDING OUT WHAT WORKS BEST

In his 2015 book 'Black Box Thinking', the British journalist, Matthew Syed, described how Unilever solved a problem with the nozzles they used to make their many brands of washing powder. To produce the washing powder, they forced chemicals through the nozzles at high pressure, collecting the powder the process produced. However, they had an ongoing struggle with the nozzles; they were inefficient and kept clogging up, costing them time and money, and reducing the quality of their product. To solve the problem they turned to their team of mathematicians; experts in physics, high pressure systems, and fluid dynamics. The experts spent a great deal of time studying the problem, developing theories and producing sophisticated equations. However, when their theories were put into practice they didn't work, the nozzles were still clogging.

Unexpectedly, it was Unilever's biologists, using an evolution-inspired, practical, hands on process, that solved the issue with the clogging nozzles. Using a more applied approach, they made small incremental changes to the nozzles and then tested them to see what worked and what didn't work. When they saw improvements they changed the nozzles further and again assessed what worked and what didn't work. They repeated this process until they produced an excellent design that worked flawlessly. They rejected many nozzles that failed on the way, but they saw each failure as a necessary part of the process to getting things right. They embraced the failures because they told them what they needed to do differently. Failing was a necessary part of the process. So they solved the problem not by developing a beautiful theoretical masterplan, but by interaction with the real world – their approach mirrored how change happens in nature.

I want you to take the same approach on the journey you will take in this book – test out the exercises for yourself and see what works best for you. When something does work, consider if you can modify it so it fits in with your values and lifestyle in a way that makes it even more effective. Don't be afraid of testing different approaches out, and don't worry, if after giving it some time, an exercise doesn't work well for you. Just see it as part of the process of finding out what does work.

The book is divided into six main parts:

The Road to Anxiety
In this part we will look at how and why anxiety develops, what it feels like, when it can be useful, and when it becomes a problem. We'll also look at the two different pathways to anxiety and consider why some of the most popular anxiety treatments are destined to fail as they only consider one of these pathways.

Step 1: Calming the Mind
This will be the start of the practical journey. It's about considering and understanding who you are, assessing how balanced your life is, and preparing you to make changes. We'll also introduce exercises that will create a solid foundation by calming the mind and preparing you for the mindfulness skills that will be introduced in the next section.

Step 2: Dealing with Anxious Thoughts and Feelings
Having created a foundation, we will now look at strategies that will help you to change your relationship with anxiety and allow you to manage uncomfortable thoughts and feelings as they arise. You'll also learn how to deal with anxiety caused by unhelpful thinking and how to handle the uncomfortable feelings we experience in stressful and challenging situations. By understanding how your thoughts and feelings work, you'll be able to create a calmer, clearer mind.

Step 3: Taking Action
Anxiety often leaves us feeling stuck and unable to take action. As a result, we often don't do the things we would like to do, and avoid taking action on many of the things we need to do, often making difficult situations even worse. In this part you'll learn how to take action when feeling anxious and discover how to build confidence in four straight-forward steps. This part finishes with a project that practically applies all of the principles and techniques you've learned so far. Life begins at the end of your comfort zone and we're going to start leaving it here.

Emergency Exercises: Managing Fight, Flight, or Freeze
This part contains some short and simple exercises that are focused on reducing the extreme symptoms of anxiety. It includes exercises that can be practised when feeling particularly anxious, stressed, or on the edge of 'losing it'. We will also outline what can be done to reduce the effects of panic attacks and how to eliminate future episodes.

Moving Forward
Now you know how to deal with your anxious thoughts and feelings, and have started to take action, it's time to think about how to weave these practices into your everyday life in a way that becomes sustainable over the long-term. In this part we will also summarise the key points in the book and look at how you can create a life that's meaningful and fulfilling.

Before You Start:
The Importance of Mindset

Recent research investigating the effect of mindset on health has demonstrated how beliefs and attitudes can change the way the body responds to physical and mental threats, and have a direct impact on our wellbeing. Studies by Harvard University psychologists Alia Crum and Ellen Langer, highlighted in Kelly McGonigal's excellent book *The Upside of Stress*[1], have demonstrated that changing the way we think about an experience can change what is happening in our bodies. The research is both remarkable and surprising, and will make you think twice about your beliefs. When I first discovered the research it completely changed the way I thought about my own anxiety.

MINDSET AND PHYSICAL HEALTH

Crum and Langer's research first came to my attention when I was preparing a health psychology module for undergraduate students in 2007. The findings of their first mindset study made me scratch my head in disbelief. The researchers recruited hotel maids to investigate if a change in mindset could lead to a change in physical health.[2] Before starting the intervention they found that two thirds of the maids believed they weren't exercising regularly. Measurements of their physical health reflected this belief: the maids' blood pressure, body weight, and waist-to-hip ratio matched those of sedentary people. This puzzled Crum and Langer because the work the maids were doing was physically strenuous, burning over 300 calories an hour (in comparison, the average office worker burns only 100 calories an hour).

So they divided the hotel maids into two groups; an experimental mindset group and a control group. The mindset group attended a talk and were given an information sheet explaining the work they were doing each day was demanding physical exercise that exceeded the Surgeon General's recommendations for an active lifestyle: pushing carts loaded with linen, lifting heavy mattresses, vacuuming, and walking from room to room. They also put posters around the group's workplace stating the same information, including detailing how many calories they burned while doing each activity. The maids in the control group were only given information about how important physical exercise is for health, but weren't told their work qualified as exercise.

At the end of the study, four weeks later, the hotel maids in the mindset group had shown some remarkable improvements in their physical health; the group's blood pressure had dropped, they had lost weight, and reduced their body fat. These changes happened with no extra physical exercise being completed inside or outside of their work and no change in diet. The control group showed no changes in physical health over the same four week period.

So the study appeared to indicate that our expectations, and beliefs about our behaviour — our mindset — can influence outcomes, or put another way, 'the effect you expect is the effect you get.'

MINDSET AND HUNGER

To test these findings further, Crum and colleagues designed a study to test if people's perceptions of how calorific a certain food is can affect their levels of fullness and hunger.[3] They gave participants two different milkshakes; one was described as an *indulgent treat that was high in calories and fat*, and the other was described as a *healthy diet shake with low calories and low fat*. However, in reality the milkshakes were exactly the same, they were just labelled differently. The researchers also measured the changes in the participants' blood levels of ghrelin — a hormone associated with hunger. When blood levels of ghrelin go down, we feel full and sated, when they rise we feel hungry.

The measurements found that when the participants believed they had drank an indulgent high calorie shake, their ghrelin levels dropped three times as much as when they thought they were drinking a low calorie shake. Remember, when ghrelin levels go down, we feel full. The participants also reported feeling more full and less hungry after the high calorie shake. So the findings weren't just based on self-reported perceptions, the different perceptions resulted in hormonal changes. So their expectations altered the levels of their hormones.

In both of these studies – the hotel maid study and the milkshake study – the participants' body responses changed when their mindset – their perceptions – changed. A change in mindset resulted in the body reacting in an adaptive, or more helpful way. Perceiving physical work as exercise helped the body experience the benefits of being active, and viewing a milkshake as a high calorific indulgence helped the body produce signals of fullness.

MINDSET AND STRESS

However, it is their latest study, published in 2015, that interested me the most. Knowing stress can be both harmful and beneficial, Crum and colleagues wondered if changing the way people thought about stress would change the way the body responded. Can mindset affect how the body experiences stress? To examine if this was the case they manipulated people's views of stress and then examined how their bodies reacted to a stressful situation.[4]

They divided participants into two groups. One group watched a three minute video presenting research that outlined the benefits of stress: how it can improve performance, make us more focused, alert, and competitive. The other group watched a three minute video that presented research outlining the negative and debilitating aspects of stress. Both videos were based on real research, because stress can indeed be both helpful and unhelpful. However, the videos were also designed to prime the perceptions of the participants into a positive or negative mindset. After watching the video both groups were subjected to tough mock interviews, with interviewers trained to give negative and critical feedback to the participants throughout.

Samples of two stress hormones were also taken from both groups before and after intervention. The hormones measured were cortisol and dehydroepiandrosterone (DHEA). Cortisol turns sugar and fat into energy and directs the body to use that energy when stressed, while also suppressing some biological functions, such as digestion and reproduction. DHEA is a neurosteroid – a hormone that helps brain grow stronger from stressful experiences. It also counters some of the effects of cortisol, as well as speeding up the repair of wounds, and improving immune function.

We need both of these hormones when experiencing stress. Each has an important part to play, so neither can be categorically stated as good or bad. However, the ratio between the hormones can influence the long-term impact of stress, especially when stress is chronic: long lasting and consistently occurring over time.

High levels of cortisol over long periods have been linked with weakened immune function and depression, but high levels of DHEA are associated with reductions in anxiety, depression, heart disease, and other diseases we associate with stress. The ratio of DHEA to cortisol is called the growth index of a stress response, and the more DHEA present, the higher the growth index. High growth indexes have been shown to help people flourish under stress; increasing resilience and helping recovery.

So to summarise, a greater ratio of DHEA to cortisol in the stress response creates a higher growth index, and a higher growth index is beneficial for the body, reducing the impact of the stress response and protecting the body from many of the diseases associated with stress.[5]

The preliminary results of the study indicated the type of video a participant watched had no effect on cortisol; this rose in both groups during the mock interview. However, there were higher levels of DHEA, and therefore a higher growth index, in the group that watched the video informing them stress was beneficial. So the results suggested viewing stress as helpful created a different biological reality, again demonstrating expectations can alter hormones and help the body to become more adaptive.

The next steps in the research were to discover if these changes in mindset were long lasting, or if they only had a temporary effect.

CHANGES IN MINDSET ARE LONG LASTING

Further studies by Crum and colleagues have gone on to show that changing a person's mindset, unlike a placebo, tends to have a long-lasting impact on their lives and is not just specific to one event. So changing an individual's mindset about stress doesn't just help them cope with the stress of a one time mock interview, but goes on to influence their beliefs and physical reactions to stress in other stressful situations over a much longer period of time. The research has also gone on to demonstrate that people who believe stress can be beneficial tend to have fewer health problems and cope better with challenges than those who see stress as harmful. It's not that they are less stressed, the research shows they are in fact just as stressed as the people who don't cope as well, but they interpret the stress response differently and are able to manage it more effectively.

Stress mindsets are powerful because they affect not just how we think, but how we act too. If we think stress is harmful, we are also more likely to become anxious and distract ourselves from dealing with stressful and problematic situations, rather than tackling them and sorting them out. So instead of dealing with the source of the anxious feelings, we focus on getting rid of them, and we sometimes do this in maladaptive ways, like turning to food, alcohol, or other substances.

On the other hand, when we see stress as beneficial, or enhancing, we don't try to distract ourselves from feeling anxious or try to avoid it, but accept it's real, and plan a strategy for dealing with the situation. People with this mindset often seek help or advice, and take steps to tackle the source of the anxiety, viewing it as an opportunity to grow and improve. So mindset changes can be thought of as catalysts; they put processes into motion that create and maintain positive changes over time.

CHANGING OUR MINDSET

People have difficulty accepting brief interventions can change a mindset because they believe meaningful problems are deep rooted and difficult to change. However, changing a mindset isn't some sort of magical manipulation, it's about educating people and showing them they have a choice about what to believe. The most successful interventions designed to change mindset have three stages:[6]

- Firstly, people are educated, learning the new point of view.
- Secondly, they then participate in an exercise that encourages them to apply the new mindset.
- Finally, they are given the opportunity to share the idea with others.

So in the case of changing an individual's mindset about stress; firstly they would learn the benefits of feeling stressed, then they would be given a chance to adopt the new mindset in a stressful situation, and finally they would be encouraged to share and explain their new mindset with others. This is exactly what happened in Crum and Langer's stress study. So in what way can anxiety and stress be beneficial?

THE BENEFITS OF STRESS

We will consider when and how anxiety can be problematic and debilitating over the next few chapters. We will also discuss the stress response in greater detail throughout the book, but having discussed how important mindset is – our beliefs about anxiety – let's first talk about how anxiety and stress can be beneficial.

The stress response is also referred to as the emergency arousal system, and the fight, flight, or freeze response. It's vital to our survival, our management of challenging situations, and how we relate to other people (more of this later). So we should see it as our friend and appreciate it. Its intention is to keep us safe from danger and help us to perform at our best when we are challenged. The stress response can be initiated by anxiety about a potentially threatening situation, as well as a reaction to being in an actual threatening situation.

The Challenge Response

Not every response we have to anxiety-inducing situations is an all or nothing fight or flight response. We have understandable stress responses when important things are at stake, but there is some nuance in our stress response. When there is a real threat to our survival we will experience the full flight, flight or freeze response, along with strong biological changes. However, when the situation is less threatening, we tend to experience a *challenge response*. The muscles and brain get more energy, heart rate increases, and adrenaline is released. All of these changes are there to help us perform better under pressure and in stressful situations: giving us a detailed focus of attention, more energy, heightened senses, and greater motivation.

Connection and Courage

An often overlooked hormone released in the stress response is oxytocin. When oxytocin is released into the bloodstream it motivates us to seek out social connection, while also raising our levels empathy, trust, and intuition. This is why, when we feel challenged or stressed, we often seek out other people to talk to or be with. Recent research has shown that contrary to most people's expectations, when people are caught up in traumatic events, such as a terror attack, they are more likely to help each other rather than act only in their best interests.[7] However, more than just seeking out social connection, oxytocin also dampens the fear response in the brain: increasing courage and suppressing the urge to fight or flee.

Learning and Recovery

Experiencing a stress response also prepares us for similar future stressful situations, and expecting to learn from stressful situations can give us a type of stress inoculation – just like vaccinations protect or inoculate us from future illness by stimulating our immune systems to develop immunity. The brain does this by using the previously mentioned DHEA, along with nerve growth factor – which is released in the stress response to increase the brain's ability to learn and change. These hormones also speed up physical and mental recovery, helping us to bounce back from challenging situations more quickly.

This is often why, for a number of hours after a stressful event, we go over it in our minds – time and time again – considering how we responded, what actions we did, and what thought processes we used. We talk to others about it and experience intense emotions of relief, shock, joy, and anger. All of this makes the experience more memorable, allowing it to change the brain in order to be better equipped to respond to similar situations in the future.

Many professionals are encouraged to practise skills, techniques, and actions in stressful situations. Footballers practise penalty kicks in front of crowds, emergency service responders practise procedures in challenging environments. Going through a stressful situation can make us better at responding in similar challenging situations. If we can see anxiety-inducing situations as opportunities to improve, grow, and become better at challenges, we are less likely to avoid or distract ourselves from them.

A GROWTH MINDSET

We've made the case that anxiety and stress can be beneficial in certain circumstances, but that is not to say the way we experience it is always helpful and we should just accept it as it is and do nothing about it. As we will find out, it also can be debilitating and overwhelming, especially when our anxiety triggers a full fight, flight, or freeze response when it's not needed. If you suffer from anxiety in this way, or are often troubled by anxious thoughts that make life difficult, the idea of anxiety being beneficial may sound ridiculous, and the suffering you've endured over time may have left you feeling hopeless. However, it isn't suffering that leads to hopelessness, it's suffering you think you can't control. This book is going to provide you with hope. Not a magical positive thinking type of hope, but a real and practical hope. So it's important you approach the following chapters with an understanding that:

1. Anxiety isn't all bad. Changing the way we think about anxiety is the first step to overcoming it.

2. Change is possible. Our abilities, skills, emotions, and behaviour are not fixed. Through learning, effort, and application, we can change, grow and transform our relationship with anxiety, and be our best selves.

The Road to Anxiety

Chapter 1
The Components of Anxiety

It's just after 6am in early May and the sun is already pouring through the bedroom curtains. I ease myself out of bed and tip-toe down the stairs so not to wake anyone up. I make a cup of coffee, give my dog – Rocket – a pat on the head as he settles down next to me, and sit down ready to write. I'm in the middle of writing this book, the one you're reading right now. While drinking my coffee I decide to have a quick look at the news before getting to work on the draft. A story about the slowing economy catches my eye and I immediately start to think about my decision to leave my job at the university the previous year. Before I can catch myself I'm imagining a scenario in which I won't have enough money to pay the mortgage, which is followed by thoughts of the house being repossessed. It probably won't happen, I think, but what if it did?

Just as I'm pondering this, Rocket – a highly strung terrier – sees our neighbour's cat jumping onto the garden fence, and as quick as a flash, jumps up against the patio door barking loudly and furiously. Startled, my whole body is activated with a surge of energy and I turn quickly to see why he's barking, knocking my arm against my cup of coffee. I react and catch the cup before it falls over, then see the cat on the garden fence. My heart is pounding, but I'm safe.

The events in the above scenario illustrate the main components of anxiety, along with the two different pathways that lead to it. This is because anxiety can be produced from two different areas of the brain; the cortex, which produces anxiety based on what we think about, and the amygdala, which reacts to what is happening in our environment. We'll discuss these two pathways in more detail later on the Chapter 3, but it would beneficial to start with the components of anxiety. If we know what our anxiety is made up of, we can reflect on what is going on inside us, make sense of our experiences, and then manage it more effectively.

Researchers and clinicians have identified three basic components of anxiety:

1. PHYSIOLOGICAL
The first of these components is physiological arousal. This is what happens when our fight, flight, or freeze reaction kicks in and adrenaline starts pumping, producing a cascade of physiological symptoms. These symptoms may include: shortness of breath, muscle tension, sweating, dizziness or light-headedness, stomach upset, tremors and twitches, headaches, and frequent urination or diarrhea. Physiological arousal can be helpful when we're in a genuinely dangerous or challenging situation, but it can also be detrimental to our physical and mental health when we respond frequently in this way to non-life-threatening situations.

2. COGNITIVE AND EMOTIONAL
The second component is the cognitive and emotional part of anxiety. This is the future-orientated thinking and fear, and the accurate and inaccurate risk appraisal. So it's ruminating about what could go wrong and how awful that will feel. It's not that

all future orientated thinking is wrong – it's important for us to think about the future and plan for what may go wrong, this is what makes us such a successful species – however, much of the time it can be inaccurate and unhelpful.

3. BEHAVIOURAL

The final basic component is the behavioural aspect of anxiety – the avoidance behaviour and rituals – in essence, the things we do in order not to feel anxious. We may avoid the anxious situation or task altogether, or distract ourselves from it with social media, alcohol, eating, or a number of other behaviours. It's understandable that we try to avoid anxiety because we find it very unpleasant. However, in avoiding anxiety we often restrict our lives, or end up causing ourselves more problems. We can sometimes, with the right mindset, respond to anxiety in a positive way, such as doing extra preparation if we feel anxious about an interview or a test, but often we respond in a way that is unhelpful.

Exercise:
Recognising the Components of Anxiety

Before reading further I'd like you to complete a quick exercise, it's only going to take a few minutes.

Step 1
Take a moment to think of something that makes you feel moderately anxious. Something real, not imagined. Maybe it's a task or job you need to do, a situation you're involved in, or an up-and-coming event that provokes some anxiety in you. Imagine you have to do that task or job right now, deal with that relationship right now, or involve yourself in that situation right now.

Step 2

Now see if can you be aware of, and identify, those three basic components of anxiety.

- Firstly, is there a physiological response? Maybe your breathing has changed, your heart is beating faster, your stomach has butterflies, or your muscles have become a little tense.

- Secondly, is there a cognitive or emotional response? Some future-orientated thinking, a scene of what could happen in the future? A feeling of fear?

- Finally is there a behavioural aspect to it? Are you thinking of ways to avoid it, put it off, or distract yourself from it?

That is all you need to do for now, be aware of the components. Later in the book we'll talk about how to manage anxiety, but it's important initially that we learn to notice it and become mindful of what is happening, rather than falling into automatic pilot. Over the following days, see if you can start to become aware of when you're feeling anxious, and when you do notice, try to identify the three components.

*

The general overall experience of anxiety is not very pleasant, if it was I'm sure you wouldn't be reading this book. We often want to get rid of anxiety as we don't enjoy experiencing these components, and some of us will go to great lengths to avoid them. If we find anxiety so troublesome, why have we evolved to experience it? What is its purpose in our lives? To understand the role of anxiety we need to take a journey into our past.

Chapter 2
Our Troublesome Brains

While modern life can intensify our anxiety, the building blocks for our struggle with anxiety can be found way back in the past with some of our earliest descendants.

There was only one goal for our early ancestors – survival – and we developed to survive above everything else. Being happy wasn't a consideration to the evolutionary forces that shaped our early behaviours; the main aim was for us to survive long enough to mate and reproduce. Life beyond survival and reproduction didn't matter. However, the instincts and intellectual abilities that helped us to survive in the past – and can still serve us well now – have also created some present day negative consequences for us as individuals. We didn't evolve to be happy, we evolved to survive. This has set us up for a number of difficulties. Why is this?

Well imagine what life was like for our very early descendants, the hominids. They were much slower than most other animals alive at the time, in comparison they had average sight and smell, and they also weren't relatively big or strong.

So in order to survive, our ancestors had to have other advantages. These came in the form of an opposable thumb and flexible fingers – that could make tools and weapons – and also, in the brain, a growing cerebral cortex. The cortex played a very important role in the survival of hominids by remembering moments of pleasure and pain. It did this in order to figure out how to maximise future pleasure and avoid future pain. This motivated our ancestors to survive, while also keeping them safe.

The cortex produces thoughts that are tailored to the demands of its environment, and the environment of our early descendants was quite different to the modern developed world we now live in. Our ancestors lived in small bands or groups, it was rare for them to meet new people, and often dangerous when they did. They also faced starvation, parasites, illness, injury, and the hazards of childbirth; and there were no medications, painkillers, medical facilities, or police to help them. This was where the human brain developed, and it was a hazardous and threatening habitat.

In this type of dangerous environment our ancestors could make two possible types of mistake: thinking they had seen a lion behind the bushes when it was actually a rock, or thinking they had seen rock behind the bushes when it was actually a lion. The cost of the first mistake was needless anxiety, while the cost of the second mistake was death. So we evolved to make the first type of mistake multiple times in order to avoid making the second mistake even once.

There may have been some happy hominids who were carefree and not continually focused on looking out for danger, but it's likely they weren't the ones that reproduced our ancestors. Their genes wouldn't have survived; they would have died before they had the chance to reproduce. So our ancestors remembered every bad thing that happened and spent much of their lives anticipating more trouble, and this is the mind we inherited from them.

Interaction of Survival Systems

Along with the cerebral cortex there are also a number of inbuilt survival systems that help to keep us safe from danger and motivated to survive, but the way these systems interact can sometimes cause us to feel anxious, stressed and unhappy.

1. THE NEGATIVITY BIAS

Research has discovered we developed what is called a 'negativity bias'.[2] So if you did ten good things today but made one mistake, it's more likely when you go to bed tonight you'll remember the one mistake – this is the negativity bias in practice. How and why does this happen?

Well there's a part of the brain shaped like an almond, called the amygdala, designed to evaluate our environmental circumstances and decide whether something is a threat or not. The amygdala reacts far more rapidly and thoroughly to negative than positive stimuli. As a result, the negative tends to contaminate the positive far more easily than the positive contaminates the negative. This is why we react more strongly to threats than positive events, why trust is easy to lose but difficult to gain, why negative political campaigns tend to dominate the media, and why we spend more time on social media criticising what we don't like or agree with rather than promoting what we love. Negativity gets people's attention more quickly and easily, and takes precedence over positive information.

The negativity bias developed in very harsh conditions, but continues in today's relatively safe environments. So we can react to relatively safe and benign conditions, such as talking to a stranger, going on a date, or making a speech, as though they are life or death situations, and very often we expect the worst.

2. THE EMERGENCY AROUSAL SYSTEM

The negativity bias also interacts with our emergency arousal system – the fight, flight or freeze response – which can be triggered by the negative thoughts we have. When triggered, the amygdala, from its central position in the brain, sends out instructions to energise the sympathetic nervous system, increasing the levels of hormones such as adrenaline and cortisol in bloodstream. This results in a number of changes in the body, including: elevated heart rate, more rapid breathing, dilated pupils, blood flow diverted away from the digestive tract to the limbs, and tensed muscles. The body is now primed for action. When this happens you may feel like your heart is pounding, your body is trembling, and your stomach and bowels are distressed.

When this reaction is needed — such as in a life saving emergency or in a very challenging environment — it's extremely helpful, but if the arousal system overreacts, it can set off a fully blown panic attack when no logical reason for fear exists. Our bodies evolved to react like this occasionally (like when we see a dangerous animal or need to run away from a group of enemies), but we don't cope very well when it's activated all day long, over weeks, months, or years. When it is, it sets us up for many anxiety related ailments, both physical and mental.

Indeed, long-term elevated cortisol levels can lower immune function and bone density; elevate blood pressure, cholesterol and body weight; increase the risk of heart disease, depression and mental illness; and interfere with learning and memory.[10] As we discussed when talking about mindset in the Introduction, changing the way we think about our stress response can minimise these negative effects and even benefit our health. However, the stress response didn't evolve to be continually activated for long periods of time, but only when needed for survival or to help us in a challenging situation.

3. SEEKING PLEASURE AND AVOIDING PAIN

As mentioned earlier, we evolved to pursue pleasure and avoid pain. This motivates us to do things that perpetuate our DNA, normally through pleasurable experiences such as sex, eating, sleeping, and finding a safe home. As a result we can get hooked on constantly seeking these things, and when we don't have the perfect conditions that allow us to experience them, or fear we could lose them, it makes us feel distressed. So we're not only impacted by immediate threats to our survival, but also the fear we won't get what we evolved to seek out, or lose what we have.

So these three survival systems do an excellent job of keeping us alive, while also pushing us to experience pleasure, but their interactions also prime us for anxiety.

The Interaction of Our Survival Systems

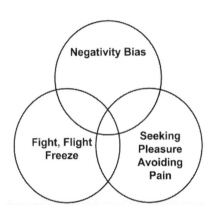

NEUROPLASTICITY
On top of these three hardwired survival systems, we have also discovered learning changes the brain, through what neurologists call *experience-dependent neuroplasticity*. Scientists used to think the brain reached maturity around the age of 25 years and then deteriorated. Now we know it's much more like a muscle, and while it ultimately weakens over our lifespan, when we use specific neural pathways in our brain, they become stronger, and if we don't, they become weaker.[11]

The principle of neuroplasticity is relatively simple: information travels throughout the brain via electrical impulses that move along nerve cells called neurons. In order for an impulse to travel from one neuron to another, it has to pass through synapses separated by an empty space called the synaptic cleft. Whenever we have a thought, a synapse fires a chemical across the cleft to another synapse, building a bridge over which the electric signal can cross, carrying the information along its charge. Every time this chemical is fired, the synapses grow closer together in order to decrease the distance the electrical impulse has to cross.

This is the brain rewiring its own circuitry, physically changing itself, to make it easier and more likely the most used synapses will share the chemical link and fire together. This makes it easier for the information to be passed on. So the repetition of signals travelling down the same pathways, through repeated behaviour and learning, reshapes the brain. This is why, in 1949, neuroscientist Carla Shatz coined the term '*Neurons that fire together, wire together*'. As a result, negative (and positive) thought patterns can deepen and become more habitual, like a riverbed that deepens over time.

With all of these evolutionarily hardwired systems operating to help us to survive, it's no wonder we so often find life difficult in the developed world. Later in the book we're going to look at interventions that were developed in response to this complex evolutionary predicament. The interventions are far-reaching in their effect on mental wellbeing because they address two challenges simultaneously:

- Firstly, they can provide insight into the patterns of the mind that create anxiety and suffering, radically changing our views of ourselves and others.

- Secondly, they can retrain the brain not to automatically respond using these instinctual patterns.

*

Now we have some understanding of why anxiety developed, how it has played a vital role in helping us survive, and why we can find it so troublesome, we will next take a closer look at the processes that take place in the brain when we experience anxiety. Understanding where the anxiety response starts is key to effectively managing our troublesome brains.

Chapter 3
The Pathways to Anxiety

At the beginning of the first chapter we mentioned that anxiety can originate from two different areas of the brain. Anxiety produced as a result of our thoughts is initiated in the **cortex**, and anxiety produced by our reaction to what is happening in our environment is initiated in the **amygdala**.

From this point on I'll refer to anxiety originating in the cortex as the *'thought pathway'* and anxiety originating in the amygdala as the *'reactive pathway'*. Everyone is capable of experiencing anxiety through both pathways, but it's important to recognise which pathway the anxiety has originated from in order to effectively manage it. We'll now summarise how each of the pathways work and how we can best manage the anxiety that originates in each one. I'd recommend the book *Rewire Your Anxious Brain* by Catherine Pittman if you are interested in reading about the pathways in greater detail.

In the personal example I gave at the beginning of the first chapter, anxiety was aroused in the thought pathway by my thoughts about having my house repossessed; and the anxiety produced by my dog barking suddenly and loudly – followed by my quick reaction to catching my cup of coffee – was a result of my amygdala reacting to the environment – the reactive pathway. Knowing the differences between the two pathways enables us to design practical interventions and exercises that are effective in changing our experience of anxiety and modifying the circuits in the brain to help us regulate it successfully.

Over the last twenty years or so, neurological research has revolutionised our knowledge of the brain structures and circuits involved in producing anxiety. Most current interventions for anxiety, such as psychotherapy or Cognitive Behavioural Therapy (CBT), are based on changing and logically disputing thoughts, and therefore target cortex-based anxiety, often only impacting the thought pathway. While they can be very effective for managing anxious thoughts, using these exercises when experiencing the reactive amygdala-based anxiety is often ineffectual, and can sometimes be detrimental. Let's look at the two pathways in more detail.

1. The Reactive Pathway

The amygdala is located centrally in the brain and involved in both pathways to anxiety. Like a built in security system, it scans the environment for any indication of danger, getting its sensory information (sights, sounds, smells, touch) from a structure in the brain called the thalamus. The thalamus sends the sensory information to both the cortex and the amygdala, but crucially, the amygdala receives this information first (see next diagram). This is because the amygdala is wired to respond rapidly to save your life; it's an evolution-based safety measure. If the amygdala recognises the information received as dangerous, it acts immediately and triggers the emergency arousal system: the fight, flight, or freeze response.

This arousal response energises the sympathetic nervous system, which produces a rapid cascade of physiological arousal, resulting in a number of changes in the body to ensure we are primed for action. This means your amygdala can react to protect you from danger before your cortex is even aware of what the danger is. This is why we can react by jumping out of the way of a speeding car or rapidly pulling back our hand when it touches a hot surface before we have time to understand what we're reacting to.

It takes a little more time for the cortex to receive this information and for us to understand what is happening. So we may quickly jump away from a tomato stem that looks like a spider, but then recover almost immediately when the information reaches the cortex, is assessed, and recognised as a harmless tomato stem. This is the same response we discussed earlier in relation to our early ancestors, it was safer for the amygdala to mistake a rock for a lion, than wait for the cortex to assess the situation before reacting. It could be the difference between life and death.

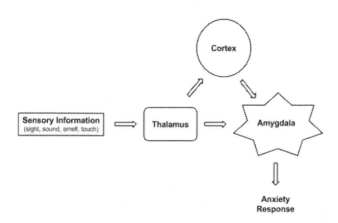

Being aware of these rapid responses initiated by the reactive pathway can help us to understand and cope with the symptoms created by the fight, flight, or freeze response, including the most extreme reaction: a panic attack. The amygdala not only reacts faster than the cortex, but there are more connections running from the amygdala to the cortex than the other way around. This enables the amygdala to hijack our thinking, overriding other responses, so there is no logical reasoning, just an automatic reaction. This is vital when saving our lives (we don't want to be able to notice the nice multi-layered shades of a lion's fur when it is running towards us) but it makes it almost impossible for us to reason away this type of anxiety and make sense of why it is happening.

So while cortex-based strategies are more popular, it is essential to also practise strategies that can counter reactive pathway anxiety and train our brain to stop responding unnecessarily in the future.

HOW THE REACTIVE PATHWAY LEARNS WHAT IS DANGEROUS

What sort of information does the amygdala respond to? Research shows we appear to be predisposed to some dangers that have helped us survive and evolve. We tend to react to snakes, insects, animals, angry faces, and contamination with little hesitation.[12] However, with training and experience, even these instinctual fears can be overcome. It's now common to have animals living with us in our houses as pets, and also for people to be able to handle snakes and spiders without fear.

In addition to these predisposed fears, the main way the amygdala learns about what is dangerous is through *emotional memories using the process of association*. These could be emotional memories you may or may not remember, as the cortex and the amygdala use completely separate memory systems. The memory system the amygdala uses doesn't contain images or verbal information, instead you experience it directly as an emotional state. This is why you sometimes may experience anxiety without really knowing why. Maybe a certain smell, location, situation, or object may make you feel anxious for no logical reason that comes to mind. This is the emotional memory of the amygdala at work.

So an object may not be threatening in itself for fear to be associated with it as the amygdala can link it to an emotional memory. If a person was involved in a car accident, and at the time of impact a pine fragrance air freshener broke open, filling the car with the smell of pine, just smelling pine in the future may make that person feel anxious, even if they do not recall why.

It can also work the other way, in that a smell, sight, object, or situation may be associated with positive feelings. A loving grandmother may have worn a certain fragrance when handling you as a baby, and now you come to associate that smell with the feeling of love and security, even though you may have no conscious recollection of your grandmother wearing that perfume or even picking you up as baby. So the reactive pathway is responsible for many of our emotional reactions, both positive and negative.

MANAGING REACTIVE PATHWAY ANXIETY

The amygdala learns through experience that something is dangerous or upsetting, so using therapies or interventions that target anxious thinking to overcome anxieties caused by the amygdala pathway aren't likely to be successful. We're focusing on the wrong pathway. So how do we learn to effectively manage amygdala-based anxiety? There are two main ways.

1. Managing Through Awareness

First of all we must recognise it's amygdala-based anxiety we're experiencing and understand that using the cortex to provide logical explanations for this type of anxiety isn't likely to help, on the contrary it can often make the anxiety worse.

A person attending a large work conference may feel their heart rate rapidly increasing, their breathing becoming more shallow, and their hands starting to shake as they enter a room full of strangers. This is the reactive pathway at work. What is the amygdala trying to protect this person from? As mentioned earlier, bumping into a group of strangers in prehistoric times was uncommon and dangerous, and there was a good chance we would be robbed, beaten or even murdered. One of the amygdala's roles is to prevent us from being prey to a predator, and it can often mistake a safe, modern-day environment, for a dangerous one.

The person attending the conference is unaware the amygdala is automatically reacting to protect them from perceived danger, and in a situation like this, the thought pathway will use the cortex to create reasons for the anxious reaction, such as *'I feel this way because I'm worried people will ignore me if I introduce myself'*, *'They all seem more competent than me, I'm likely to make a fool of myself if I start talking to someone.'* The more the person focuses on these logical cortex-based explanations for their anxiety, the more anxiety they will create, adding to the original problem. So being aware of the amygdala's ability to take charge is essential.

If we find ourselves in a situation like this we need to be aware our amygdala is trying to protect us, but what we're experiencing isn't life threatening. In the previous example, the conference may have been important, even crucial for the person's career, but it was unlikely to mean life or death. So the person must accept the physical reactions were due to the amygdala trying to protect them. While these reactions would be helpful if they needed to fight or flee, this isn't a dangerous situation, and coming up with logical explanations for it will only add to the anxiety. This is why, when people experience panic attacks, having someone logically explain why they shouldn't be panicking doesn't help. They're talking to a cortex that is switched off or completely overpowered by the amygdala.

So recognise your amygdala is trying to protect you, but it can often be wrong. You don't want your thinking to add fire to the flames. We need to recognise when the amygdala is misreading the situation and sounding the alarm for no reason. I'll explain how we can quieten these thoughts from the cortex and reduce their influence later, in *Step 2: Dealing with Anxious Thoughts and Feelings*. Also remember if your reaction isn't overwhelmingly strong, it's likely to be a challenge response, and the challenge response can help us to perform better in challenging circumstances.

Unfortunately, awareness that the situation is not dangerous and it's just your amygdala kicking in and raising the alarm won't always remedy the situation and stop an overwhelming response. However, awareness is a key first step. In some situations, a further successful approach is to use deep breathing techniques or to engage in physical activity; these techniques can engage the parasympathetic nervous system and bring you out of the fight, flight, or freeze response, calming the mind. We go through these and other effective exercises in more detail in *Emergency Exercises: Managing Fight, Flight, or Freeze*.

2. Managing by Learning Through Experience

In order to further reduce or eliminate unhelpful amygdala-based anxiety, you have to use the language of the amygdala rather than the cortex, and that means learning through experience. If, for example, you want to change the amygdala's anxiety response to dogs, you must activate the memory circuits that relate to dogs, and only then can new connections be made and the amygdala taught to respond differently. If you want to change the amygdala's anxiety response to social situations, you must activate the memory circuits that relate to socialising.

We mentioned experience-dependent neuroplasticity earlier on in the chapter, and it is this process that allows the brain to make new connections, alter the circuitry, and change the amygdala's future responses.

People will, understandably, often try to avoid these challenging and anxiety-inducing situations, but avoiding them stops the amygdala from forming new connections and responding differently. The amygdala tries to preserve learned emotional reactions by avoiding exposure to the triggers. This decreases the likelihood of any neural changes or the anxiety being eliminated. By exposing ourselves to situations or objects that make us anxious, but challenging that association – by realising that nothing bad happens – we can develop new connections in the amygdala that compete with and eventually overpower those that create fear and anxiety.

If we can start to see anxiety-inducing situations as an opportunity to learn, change, and rewire our neural pathways, we can motivate ourselves to confront them. Although difficult, if we nurture an opportunity mindset, and understand that exposing ourselves to the anxiety that arises will produce positive neuroplastic changes, we can grasp the courage to face our fears and become unstuck. We'll address how to take action despite feeling anxiety and fear in *Step 3: Taking Action.*

2. The Thought Pathway

When we think of anxiety, we normally associate it with cortex-based anxiety, the type of anxiety created by anxious thinking. We're more consciously aware of this type of anxiety and can recognise it in our thoughts and feelings. This is because the cortex is more directly under our control than the amygdala. As a result, we're able to train ourselves to be aware of, interrupt, and change anxious thoughts and images, and therefore reduce our anxiety. However, this isn't always easy, as we develop longstanding patterns of thinking and ingrained habits.

The cortex can influence our anxiety in two main ways. Firstly, as described earlier, it can worsen anxiety originated in the amygdala by creating unhelpful and inaccurate reasons for our anxious feelings, and secondly, it can independently initiate unnecessary anxiety using thoughts and images.

HOW THE CORTEX INITIATES ANXIETY
The cortex can initiate unnecessary anxiety using thoughts and images in two main ways.

1. Firstly, by interpreting neutral or harmless sensory information (sights, sounds, smells, touch) provided to it by

the thalamus as threatening, and then sending this information onto the amygdala to produce anxiety.

For example, it's late in the evening and your telephone rings. You may immediately start to wonder why someone is calling you so late. *It's bad news, something awful has happened, maybe a family member has been involved in an accident?* Your cortex has taken this sensory information, created distressing thoughts, and sent a message to the amygdala to produce anxiety. You answer the phone to hear the voice of a friend asking you if you'd like to meet tomorrow for lunch and your anxiety subsides.

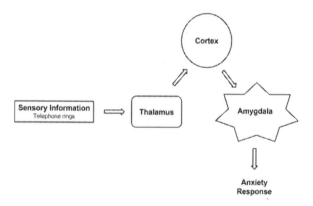

2. The second way the cortex initiates anxiety using thoughts and images, is by independently producing it's own distressing thoughts, without receiving sensory information.

You're due to travel abroad in a few days' time and start to imagine your first flight being delayed and then missing the connection to your second flight. Your cortex sends this information onto your amygdala and an anxiety response is triggered, even though there has been no sensory information provided about your flight being delayed. The amygdala responds to imaginary information in the same way it responds to a real situation, so anxiety brought about by thoughts and images created in the cortex is just as strong as the anxiety you will experience from a real and live situation or threat.

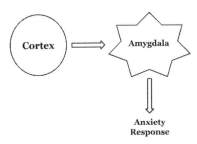

We often worry in this way, hoping the rumination will lead to a solution or will help to guard us against future negative events. We can sometimes come up with novel solutions through worrying, but rarely do. More often than not we just strengthen the neural pathways in the cortex that create worry. Due to neuroplasticity, whatever you devote a lot of time thinking about in great detail is more likely to be strengthened, creating a vicious circle.

MANAGING THOUGHT PATHWAY ANXIETY

There are a number of key skills we can learn to help us effectively manage anxious thinking. Remember, in the thought pathway, the cortex initiates anxiety in one of two ways; by interpreting neutral sensory information as dangerous, and sending this information to the amygdala to produce anxiety; or by creating anxious thoughts and feelings on it's own, without sensory information, and again, sending this information to the amygdala to produce anxiety.

So we need to learn to manage unhelpful thoughts and images in a way that will eliminate the anxiety response of the amygdala or greatly reduce its strength. This in turn will enable us to take control of our behaviour and engage fully with our actions, rather than allowing our anxiety to lead the way.

Before we outline these keys skills, let's investigate some of the other, more common solutions we are told can help reduce negative thoughts. The advice often tells us to:

- Challenge or dispute the thoughts by looking for evidence to demonstrate they aren't true.
- Replace negative thoughts with positive thoughts.
- Distract ourselves from these thoughts.

You may have tried one or more of these strategies before, and if so, you may have recognised some common problems with these approaches:

- They require a lot of effort and energy and can divert you from your original intention.
- They focus your mind on the negative thoughts.
- They only tend to give you temporary relief before your mind comes up with new negative thoughts.
- When you leave your comfort zone to enter a challenging situation they don't work.

If these methods don't work as long-term strategies, what's the alternative? Well, there's a radically different way of responding to negative thoughts that may seem counterintuitive.

The approach comes from Acceptance and Commitment Therapy (often abbreviated to ACT) — an evidenced-based psychological intervention that uses acceptance and mindfulness strategies to overcome anxiety and manage stress.[13] ACT suggests we can reduce the influence of negative thoughts and anxious feelings without trying to get rid of them. This method works even though it makes no effort whatsoever to reduce, challenge, eliminate, or change negative thoughts. Why? Because it starts from the assumption that negative thoughts are not inherently problematic.

In his book, *The Happiness Trap*, leading ACT practitioner Dr Russ Harris, explains that negative thoughts are only considered problematic if *we get caught up in them, give them all of our attention, treat them as the absolute truth, allow them to control us, or get in a fight with them.* When we do get caught up in our thoughts, give them all of our attention, and consider them to be the absolute truth, we're considered to be FUSING with them. When two things fuse together they become joined together as one. When we're caught up in our thoughts in this way we are cut off or disconnected from what is happening right in front of us, and this makes it difficult to engage with our environment. Our anxious thoughts become our reality and dominate our behaviour.

*

The ACT approach teaches three key skills to help us effectively manage cortex-based anxiety: defusion, expansion, and engagement. We'll briefly outline these skills below and then go back to them later on in the book to explain how we can practically apply them.

1. Defusion

To counteract unhelpful thoughts, we can defuse, or separate, from them. When we defuse from thoughts we become aware they are nothing more or less than words and pictures, and can have little or no effect on us, even if they are true.

As an analogy, imagine you're driving a bus, while all the passengers (thoughts) are noisily chattering, being critical, or shouting out directions. You can allow them to shout, but choose not to engage with them, keeping your attention focused on the road ahead. If you turn around and start arguing with the passengers, you may have to stop the bus, or become distracted and make a wrong turn. So you keep driving, allowing them to shout, but safe in the knowledge they can't hurt you. You defuse from them.

2. Expansion

When our cortex provides us with unhelpful thoughts we will often experience uncomfortable feelings as a result. We normally do our best to avoid these feelings or sensations, we try to distract ourselves from them, or get rid of them. However, we can learn to deal with them effectively by using expansion – this is the ability to open up and make room for emotions, sensations, and feelings.

So we accept they are there, and allow them to pass through without having an impact on our behaviour. When we experience anxious feelings, we don't battle with them, but we accommodate them and allow them to come and go in their own time. It doesn't mean we want them, like them, or approve of them, but we just stop investing our time and effort in fighting them. The more space we can give the difficult feelings, the smaller their influence and impact on our lives.

3. Engagement

The next step is engaging with experiences, tasks, and situations, despite unhelpful thoughts and uncomfortable feelings. Engagement is being present and actively involved in what we are doing – not lost in our thoughts. Being anxious is not a problem, but disengaging from our experience is.

The more we focus on unhelpful thoughts and unpleasant feelings, the more we disconnect from the present moment. This particularly tends to happen with anxiety; we get hooked on stories about the future, about how things might go wrong, and how badly we're going to handle them. We don't have to be connected to the present moment all the time, but it is particularly useful to do so in a number of situations, particularly when anxiety is diverting us away from our desired behaviour.

We will get into the detail and practicalities of defusion, expansion, and engagement in *Step 2: Dealing with Anxious Thoughts and Feelings*, and also go through a number of different of exercises in order to see what works best for you.

*

In these first three chapters we've discussed how and why anxiety develops, described the pathways it uses, and outlined how we can start to manage our anxiety. Before starting the practical journey and beginning the exercises, we're first going to raise awareness of how anxiety can progress in a way that seriously impacts our lives.

Chapter 4
Anxiety Disorders

Everyone experiences anxiety from time to time. It can often be situation specific – if we're facing a difficulty at work, taking an exam, or making an important decision – or sometimes there are just periods in our lives when we feel a little more anxious than at other times. However, sometimes anxiety can feel more permanent and affect nearly every part of our lives. How do we go from temporary or situation-specific anxiety to developing an anxiety disorder?

Escape Avoidance Learning

Most anxiety disorders develop through what psychologists call Escape Avoidance Learning, which follows this general pattern:

1. Situation.
Let's say something happened to me involving popcorn when I was a child. Maybe I nearly choked on some popcorn, or someone bullied me and tipped popcorn over my head. I had suppressed it, as when I was younger it was scary and painful. Now, much later on in life, I visit the cinema. I'm queuing for

tickets in the lobby and I can smell popcorn.

2. Anxiety
The smell of popcorn may be enough to bring up some sense of anxiety, as this is how associational memory works. It just takes a small trigger to be able to connect us back to something that was difficult or unpleasant.

3. Unpleasant feelings
I find the anxiety unpleasant, especially if I'm having some kind of physiological response (heart beating more rapidly, shallow breathing). I may feel like I'm going to have a panic attack.

4. Leave situation
I want to take steps to get rid of the unpleasant feeling, so I decide I'm going to get away from the situation by leaving the lobby, or I may even leave the cinema altogether.

5. Anxiety goes
Once outside in the car park I start to feel better and notice a reduction in my anxiety.

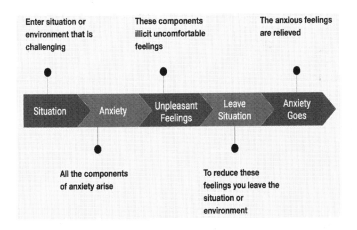

NEGATIVE REINFORCEMENT

As I managed to find relief from my anxiety by leaving the situation, I'm more likely to repeat this behaviour in the future. This is called *negative reinforcement* – the reinforcement that comes from removing an unpleasant experience. So the next time I go to the cinema and smell popcorn, I'll be more likely to do the same thing because it feels good to have the negative experience stop. This can then also extend to other situations; I may start avoiding the post office and shopping in the high street. In extreme cases this can lead to fully blown agoraphobia.

Even though the behaviour may not develop into something as serious as agoraphobia, most of us develop these little patterns around things we're afraid of, and start to avoid situations that make us feel anxious. This is then negatively reinforced, and causes limiting and problematic behaviour. We don't face our fears; we avoid them or distract ourselves from them. So how is anxiety like this normally treated?

Exposure and Response Prevention

In the 1980s a number of universities, particularly in the United States, started exploring interventions for anxiety and phobias created by specific situations.[14] A number of them experimented treating people with snake phobias to investigate and illustrate how anxiety caused by Escape Avoidance Learning can be treated. The interventions were generally designed using the following pattern:

1. The participants would arrive at the university and be told by a researcher that a snake is locked in a cage in a room some distance away.

2. Then, in the early days of this research, a relaxation method called 'reciprocal inhibition' was performed. This involved the participant being trained to reduce their anxiety using a muscle

relaxation technique. However, later on in the research it was discovered this step wasn't necessary, and participants were encouraged to just stay with the experience and allow the anxiety to be there until it went by itself.

3. With the snake still in a distant room, the researcher talked to the participant, described the snake, answered any questions, and then just waited until nothing happened and the anxiety started to decline.

4. The snake was then moved to a closer room and the participant would be given time to calm down. Step by step, the snake was moved closer, until it was brought into the same room and put in front of the participant.

5. Eventually the participant would handle the snake.

It was discovered if you repeat this exercise a number of times, the person would eventually lose their snake phobia. The anxiety response became extinguished because the participant experienced nothing terrible happened. This approach has since been found to work for nearly all phobias. This is an example of the amygdala learning from experience. It works by activating the memory circuits that cause the anxiety, and then allowing learning to rewire the neural pathways and eliminate or reduce the anxiety response.

Often, when people seek treatment for anxiety, they aren't initially interested in 'handling the snake'. They don't want the treatment to feel uncomfortable, or have to face their fears. People tend to want to get rid of the anxious feelings without feeling discomfort, but there is no magic bullet for treating anxiety. Like the people who handled the snake, this book focuses on teaching us to increase our capacity to bear the anxiety and to change our relationship with the experience.

*

When we use specific interventions and mindfulness-based exercises to treat our anxiety, research indicates they can go further than improving our present moment experience of anxiety. With consistent practice we can create a solid foundation, and by doing this we can change the structure and functioning of our brain in ways that benefit us beyond just managing our anxiety. In the next part we'll begin to look at how we start to build this foundation, along with interventions that can have a profound effect on the brain.

Step 1:
Calming the Mind

Chapter 5
Getting to Know Yourself

This chapter is the start of the practical journey this book will take you on. It's about considering and understanding who you are, assessing how balanced your life is, and preparing you to make changes. Although you may be keen to start tackling anxious thoughts and feelings immediately, it's important you first build a foundation that will hold you steady when faced with the challenge of changing your relationship with your anxiety and taking action. The exercises in this chapter are about taking a step back and assessing who you really are, how you live your life, and considering if you could change it for the better.

Who Are You?

Research suggests when we affirm our most deeply held values — the best parts of our authentic selves – before entering into a potentially threatening or challenging situation, we can reduce our anxiety, become less defensive, and more open and authentic in our behaviour. By spending a little time reflecting on, and perhaps writing, about who we think we are, we can reduce our hormonal anxiety and be more present and effective in challenging environments. The studies have shown when people write about their authentic selves before entering a potentially anxious situation, they go on to have significantly lower levels of cortisol – a hormone we release when we feel under stress – than people who don't.[15]

This is not about psyching ourselves up and exclaiming 'I'm the best!' or 'I'm a winner!' in the way we traditionally think about expressing positive affirmations. It's more about appreciating our best selves emerge when we have full access to our values, traits, and strengths, and know we can express them through our actions. In other words, it's understanding who we truly are and having the confidence to be authentic. These types of affirmations help us to believe in and clarify our own stories. This allows us to trust who we are will come through naturally in what we say and do.

In the middle of writing this chapter, while on one of my daily dog walks, I listened to a podcast presented by the rapper Scroobious Pip (real name David Meads), in which he interviewed the author Jon Ronson.[16] They were both talking about their experiences with anxiety (Ronson has written in great detail about his paralysing levels of anxiety), and Scroobious Pip remarked he had lost confidence when a relationship ended out of the blue. He described how, during this period of anxiety, he spent a week writing and recording a song (that wasn't released commercially). Pip explained how this process reminded him of who he really is, and what his values and strengths are. He said the project helped him to recover his confidence. This is what we are going to do in the following exercise; remind ourselves of who we really are, what we value, and what is important to us.

It's important we don't just reflect on our values without taking practical steps to try to fully understand them. We can do this by writing about them. Writing is a powerful exercise because it serves to clarify our thoughts and feelings in a way reflection alone is unable to. In the act of writing, ideas emerge and are shaped, and this gives us a clearer understanding of who we are.

Foundational Exercise 1: Who Are You?

Step 1

Below is a list of common core values. Choose one or two values you feel are most central to your identity, closest to the core of who you are. The list is just to help you reflect, so you don't have to choose from the list if you know of values you possess that aren't listed.

Dependable	Loyal	Efficient
Inspiring	Reliable	Committed
Adventurous	Passionate	Serving
Creative	Motivated	Respectful
Consistent	Humorous	Positive
Hardworking	Honest	Witty
Respected	Educated	Loving
Fit	Courageous	Fun-loving
Innovative	Open-minded	Kind
Athletic	Optimistic	Nurturing

Core value 1: _____

Core value 2: _____

Step 2

Then, write a short note on why these values are important to you and a particular time when they proved to be important. A person who deeply values being humorous might write:

"Being funny around others is important to me. I believe we all would be better off if we sometimes took life a bit less seriously. I really enjoy making people laugh, it makes me feel good and it comes easily to me. I remember being out with my colleagues from work and we had all been really stressed, but I managed to find humour in how difficult things were at the time and we all ended up laughing. It really broke the ice and we had a great night."

Core value 1 _____ is important to me because:

Core value 1 _____ proved to be important when:

Core value 2 _____ is important to me because:

Core value 2 _____ proved to be important when:

Notice you only need to affirm your personal core values —not values or abilities that are relevant to any specific task you need to do, or any challenge you are facing. So for example, if you have an up and coming job interview, don't try to convince yourself you'll be successful at the job interview by choosing values you think are related to the interview or job. The key to this exercise working is knowing who you are and being comfortable and assured with that.

I'd suggest repeating this exercise every so often, especially when you're facing an anxious situation or challenge. You could also try a more creative way of reflecting on your core values and strengths, by undertaking a project or task you feel expresses who you really are, much like Scroobious Pip did in the example I described above.

WHAT IF I DON'T LIKE MY VALUES OR WANT TO CHANGE THEM?

Being unsure of our values, or feeling we don't like them, is a good indication our true values are the ones we would like to have – the values we aspire to. Just because we currently don't behave in a way that is consistent to those values doesn't mean we don't hold them or can't develop them. They are hidden and need uncovering. If this is the case for you, when you try the exercise above, choose the values you would like to have – the ones that make you the type of person you would like to be.

If you're still struggling to discover your true values, it may be helpful to heed the advice of Warren Buffett, one the world's most generous philanthropists, and a very successful businessman. When addressing Seattle college students in 1998, Buffett suggested in order to nurture successful values and habits, the students should look to role models.

He told them if they wanted to live a purposeful and successful life, they should think of the person they admired the most, write down what it is they admire about them, and then aim to emulate their values and qualities. He also suggested the students should bring to mind a person they can stand the least, write down the qualities and values that turn them off that person, and avoid practising them at all costs. Buffet's message tells us that with awareness, intention, and practice, we can develop the values, qualities, and habits of those we admire, and avoid the ones of those we dislike.

*

Avoiding Exhaustion and Increasing Energy

When things get busy and we're not leading a balanced life, we often tend to let go of the things or activities that nourish us, and instead focus on what seems more important or pressing at the time. However, without the things that nourish us, stress increases and we give up more and more of the activities that replenish us. When this happens we're only left with work, chores, difficult challenges, or other stressors that really deplete our resources, and we can become exhausted or burnt out. Our lives become narrow and we get stuck in, what stress researchers call, an exhaustion funnel.[17] It's easy to get sucked into this process because we often have pressing demands, and when we do, the more pleasurable things in life tend to seem optional and are easier to give up.

However, despite feeling like we have no choice, we simply have too much to do, or we don't have the energy to do other things, it is vital we balance our lives during these times, or at the very least spend time on activities that nourish us. Although it may feel counterintuitive at the time, in order to do the other things well and to maintain our energy, we need to make time for replenishment and nourishment. This will give us the extra time, energy, and perspective needed for the challenging parts of our lives.

If you're unconvinced that resting and doing things that nourish you is a good idea during busy periods, I'd like to point you in the direction of some research demonstrating why a balanced life is both more enjoyable and productive.

Firstly, scientific evidence has emphasised **rest aids decision making**. Research by Dutch psychologist Ap Dijksterhuis (I can't pronounce it either), suggests actively trying to work through a number of decisions, particularly when tired, will lead to a worse outcome than going through all the relevant information and then taking a break, or moving on to something else.[18] During rest periods, the subconscious mind is able to sift through lots information and this helps us to make clearer, more helpful decisions. Personally, some of my best ideas and most helpful decisions have come to me when I have been out walking my dog in the countryside, *after* periods of intense work.

Secondly, research has demonstrated **rest replenishes our resources and helps us to work more effectively**. Attention Restoration Theory (ART) – an area of academic research that investigates our ability to maintain attention over time – suggests concentration is limited and we can exhaust our supply of focused attention. When this happens we're unable to work effectively or to concentrate properly.

Scientists involved in ART research suggest we should take regular breaks or switch activities when our attention is tiring. Particularly recommended is taking a break in nature. This is because there are normally less obstacles around in open spaces and therefore less decisions to be made, enabling us to switch off more completely.[19] However, if taking a break in nature is not possible, we can still be more effective at stressful tasks just by ensuring we take the time to rest, or switch to an activity we enjoy, especially something that gives us a break from concentrating or focusing intensely.[20]

Finally, **work we do when tired or depleted tends to be of very low quality**. Recent research has indicated we have a limited capacity to do work that is difficult and demanding, especially tasks that require our attentional resources.[21] Studies have shown more often than not, the activities or work we do when we are feeling tired or depleted will be substandard, or at least certainly not our best work.

Additionally, trying to work when depleted often results in errors that have to be corrected at a later time, or completely redone. So staying up late to finish a report for work when feeling tired and depleted will often result in low quality work that has to be corrected or redone the following day. So when extremely busy, while we think we must keep on going, we cannot afford a break or the time to do an enjoyable activity, we can actually save time in the long-term by taking the time to nourish ourselves.

THE HIDDEN POWER OF MIRROR NEURONS: THE COMPANY YOU KEEP

When we're considering activities and situations that nourish or deplete us we should also reflect on the impact our social relationships can have on us. In the late 1980s, by reaching for his lunch, an Italian academic made a remarkable and unexpected discovery about how the behaviours and emotions of others can directly impact on us.

Giacomo Rizzolatti and his colleagues had implanted electrodes into the brains of a number of macaque monkeys in order to study their brain activity while they performed various motor actions, including clutching food. One day, as a researcher reached for his own food while glancing at the feedback on his computer screen, he noticed neurons beginning to fire in the premotor cortex of one of the monkeys — the area that showed activity when the animals made a similar hand movement. How could this be happening when the monkey was just sitting still, not reaching out to grab food, but just watching him?

This accidental revelation led to the discovery of mirror neurons – a distinct class of brain cells that fire not only when an individual performs an action, but also when the individual observes someone else make the same movement. Further research into the workings of mirror neurons demonstrated this effect goes beyond motor movement. We now know when we see someone else experiencing an emotion, whether it be positive or negative, our brain 'tries out' that same emotion to imagine what the other person is going through.[22] It does this by trying to fire the same neural pathways in our own brains so we can attempt to relate to the emotion we're observing.

This is the way in which we experience empathy and can get caught up in both the positive and negative emotions of others; from angry mob mentality, to the solidarity of grief during and after tragedies. It also means we are directly impacted by the attitudes and beliefs of those we spend most time with. So if we're continually influenced by critical, cynical, fearful, and pessimistic attitudes, we're continually firing those synapses in our brain, rewiring it towards anxiety, fear and pessimism; rather than peace, confidence and optimism.

So when we're evaluating our lives and considering how best to balance the activities that nourish and deplete us, we should also take into consideration the company we keep and whether we can take steps to change this, and if not, consider what can we do to improve things. This is not to say we shouldn't be there for friends who are having a hard time; those who need an empathetic ear or help to work through a difficult situation. I'm also not suggesting we can never be critical, or never talk about our anxiety, fears or worries; as positive change usually requires critical thought. Only that we should consider who we consistently spend time with and are influenced by.

Foundational Exercise 2: Balancing Life

Step 1: List your daily activities
Draw a table like the one below, and in the lefthand column make a list of between 1 to 15 typical activities you do most weeks. Then state which ones nourish you by putting an N in the righthand column, and similarly which ones deplete you by putting a D in the righthand column.

By nourishing, we mean an activity that lifts your mood, gives you energy, or makes you feel calm and centred. By depleted we mean an activity that drains you, takes away your energy, and makes you feel tense. There are no right or wrong answers, what may be nourishing for you may be depleting for someone else and vice-versa.

Typical Activities	Nourishing (N) Depleting (D)
1. E.g. *Constantly checking my email*	D
2. E.g. *Going for a walk*	N
3. E.g. *Checking the news often*	D

Step 2: Redress the balance
There may be some depleting activities you can immediately stop, eliminate, or do less of, and also some nourishing activities you can do more of. Go carefully through the list and make a note of those activities, both depleting and nourishing, you can change. Don't provide any detail of how you will do it at this stage, just put a mark next to the activity. You can also consider and make a note of any new activities you don't currently do but know from past experience are nourishing for you.

What about unavoidable activities?

There will be some depleting activities you cannot change, especially not immediately (e.g. work, dealing with difficult housemates). If there are depleting activities on your list that are unavoidable, there are a few different approaches you can use:

• First of all, while you may not be able to completely avoid some depleting activities, you can try you best to nudge these depleting activities down, and the nourishing activities up. Some small, subtle changes, making the balance a little better. Think about ways you could do this.

- Secondly, you can try approaching the depleting activities in a different way. Instead of wishing them away, try being fully present with them, even if you find them boring or unpleasant. You don't have to do this for all unavoidable depleting activities, but try doing it with some and see how you feel.

Step 3: Commit to the changes

Now it's time for you to think about how to alter and commit to the changes that will improve your life balance. Write down five ways in which you can practically change things. Don't worry if you can't think of five straightaway, write down the others when they come to you at a later time.

It's important you focus on small, doable changes, not life changing activities. So don't include, 'Move to Hollywood', 'Run a marathon', or 'Marry Brad Pitt', but focus on small changes, like the examples below. These small changes are a crucial part of the practice.

I will alter the balance of nourishing and depleting activities by...
E.g. *Checking my emails only twice a day at 10am and 4pm*
E.g. *Going for a 15 minute walk during my lunch hour and 30 minute walk on the weekend*
E.g. *Checking the news once or twice a day only*

At first, you may not be aware of what activities nourish or deplete you, so it may be a case of trial and error. Be aware of this and be open to having some of your preconceived ideas challenged.

We can often think some activities are enjoyable, but when we really consider how we feel after them, we realise they deplete us and vice-versa. For example, I used to build periods of internet surfing into my day because I thought I found it enjoyable and relaxing, but when I started to monitor and be aware of how I really felt during and after various activities, I realised it often left me feeling tired, unsettled, frustrated, and mildly anxious. Conversely, I used to think mowing my lawn was a depleting activity, but after some reflection, I realised it often left me with a feeling of satisfaction and had the effect of calming my mind.

Review your activity lists every so often, particularly if you start to feel life is becoming busy, stressful and unbalanced, and consider if you need to make any further changes.

What we do with our time and how that affects our energy levels and mood is crucial to our mental wellbeing. Our energy levels have a huge impact on the way we feel, how well we can handle our emotions, how prepared we feel for challenges, and how effectively we can perform a number of tasks and activities. So it's vital these foundations are in place when we are making changes to our lives.

*

Next we will look at some exercises that calm the mind and help us to understand our thinking patterns more clearly, enabling us to make better decisions and feel more rested and peaceful.

Chapter 6
Calming the Mind

Earlier in the book we talked about the two different pathways to anxiety; the *reactive pathway*, which is amygdala-based, and the *thought pathway*, which is cortex-based. The exercises in this chapter are beneficial for both pathways and will start to prepare you for the mindfulness skills that will be introduced in *Step 2: Dealing with Anxious Thoughts and Feelings*. They have also been designed to build on the foundational exercises included in the previous chapter. Firstly, by raising awareness of our thought patterns and therefore giving us a clearer understanding of who we are; and secondly, by calming the mind and consequently providing additional help in managing energy levels.

Mindfulness

I'm sure many of you will have heard of mindfulness before, in fact you may have even rolled your eyes when you first glanced at this subtitle, I certainly would have done so a number of years back. One of the most popular mindfulness practices – meditation – has become increasingly popular in the western world over the last ten years or so. Its benefits have been championed in nearly every area of life, from business and leadership settings, to education and mental health. The blanket coverage of meditation and its perceived links with spirituality, religion, and later, business performance, put me off trying it for a long time. Further to this, nearly every time I heard a talk about meditation, or listened to a guided meditation, it was nearly always accompanied by the sound of panpipes in the background. I just felt it wasn't for me.

However, after years of researching mental health treatments and interventions for my university health psychology class, I was eventually won over by the science and came to understand that meditation, along with a number of other mindfulness practices, is a very effective method of mental training.

We mentioned experience-dependent neuroplasticity earlier, explaining we now we see the brain as more like a muscle that can be changed with exercise, and are beginning to understand what we do with our attention really matters. Our brains are plastic, meaning neurons can change how they interact with experience, and neural pathways can be strengthened or weakened depending on how much they are used. So whenever we engage in a repeated behaviour it can lead to changes in our brain structure. For example, studies have shown if you practise juggling, you'll increase the grey matter in the areas of your brain associated with visual motion.[23]

. While we are just beginning to learn about neuroplasticity, there is a gathering field of evidence indicating that specific mindfulness practices can change our brain function and structure in very beneficial ways. Let's take a look at these changes a little more closely.

Brain Function

Neurobiological research on mindfulness practices has testified to various changes in brain functioning – how well the brain performs certain tasks. Some of the most prominent changes have been documented in three areas in particular: attention, age-related cognitive decline, and emotional control.

ATTENTION

Control over where we direct our attention is key to being able to manage our emotions and behaviour. Research has demonstrated a number of improvements in brain function in various types of attention.[24a]

- These include improvements in *alerting* – becoming aware of a stimulus – like a horn honking.

- Positive changes have also been discovered in *sustained attention* – our ability to follow a stimulus over time – such as focusing for a long period of time on a task that needs to be completed.

- Improvements have also been found in *conflict monitoring* – remaining focused despite distractions trying to pull our attention away – such as continuing to be able to concentrate on writing despite being tempted to check phone notifications.

AGE-RELATED COGNITIVE DECLINE

The practices have also been shown to stave off and slow down normal *age-related cognitive decline* in the areas of [24b]:

- Short-term memory – our capacity for remembering information in an active, readily available state for a short period of time. Such as remembering the drinks of everyone in your group while making an order at the bar.

- Perceptual speed – the ability to process information quickly and accurately, particularly under the pressure of time – it includes how quickly and accurately we can recognise and compare numbers, letters, objects, pictures, or patterns.

- Executive functioning – a mix of many of our cognitive skills, including the mental processes that enable us to plan, focus, remember instructions, and multitask successfully – we use executive functioning to filter distractions, prioritise tasks, set and achieve goals, and control impulses.

EMOTIONAL CONTROL

Finally, research has shown that meditative practices can help us to take charge of our emotions by:

- Dampening amygdala activation both in the short-term and long-term, making anxious responses less reactive.[25]

- Reducing the fight, flight, or freeze response by activating the parasympathetic nervous system. This calms down anxious thinking and reduces the physiological anxiety response in the body.[26]

So the practice can have an immediate impact as well as a long-term cumulative effect on anxiety, and it also raises awareness of the chattering cortex, making it an excellent foundational exercise.

Brain Structure

There have also been a number of research studies by Sara Lazar and her Harvard University colleagues, documenting how mindfulness practices change the physical structure of the brain.[27]

- Ageing is normally related to *cortical thinning*, — losing grey matter in the prefrontal cortex. This is why, when we get older, it's more difficult to work out complex problems and remember things. Losing grey matter when we age is normal, but compared to people of the same age, studies have shown people who meditate have thicker anterior insulae, sensory cortices, and prefrontal cortices. Fifty year old meditators have been shown to have the same amount of grey matter as twenty five year olds. These three regions are also all thought to be involved with integrating emotional and cognitive processes, so they help us manage and understand our emotions more effectively and improve the quality of our thinking.

  The opposite development – decreased volume of grey matter – has been strongly associated with several clinical disorders, including post traumatic stress disorder, social anxiety, specific phobias, and schizophrenia.

- Changes have also been demonstrated in an area of the brain called the *hippocampus*, which is involved in learning, memory, and emotion regulation. Studies have shown participants who completed an eight week mindfulness course, increased grey matter concentration within the left hippocampus. Conversely, it gets smaller in people who suffer from depression and anxiety; and stress also appears to shrink it.

- Research has revealed positive changes in an area of the brain called the *temporo-parietal junction*, which is located just above the ear. It is involved in perspective taking, empathy, and also compassion.

- Interestingly, changes have also been found in, our friend, the *amygdala*, but studies indicate a decrease in grey matter for those practising mindfulness. During an eight week mindfulness programme, the more stress reduction reported, the smaller the amygdala became.

Meditation

So when done consistently, mindfulness practices, and meditation in particular, can help us to manage our emotions, alter brain structure and function, and positively change our behaviour. Despite these benefits, many people are still put off from starting meditation or find it difficult to continue with the practice after a few attempts. Let's look at some of the difficulties or blocks people encounter when attempting to start or continue with meditation.

- Some people are deterred by the spiritual or religious connotations of meditation (and mindfulness in general), but need not be. While some religious or spiritual people do meditate, meditation is not a religion, many atheists and agnostics also meditate. Meditation doesn't have to be a religious practice, and the meditations included in this book are written as mental training exercises.

- Many people think meditation takes up a lot of time, but this isn't necessarily the case. True, you may have heard stories of Tibetan monks meditating for up to 16 hours a day, but the research shows a daily practice from any time between five to twenty minutes can have a positive impact on mental wellbeing. You do have to be patient and persistent to reap the benefits, but you will also find the practice brings a clear headedness and peace that can help you to spend the time you do have more effectively.

- People will often remark they cannot meditate because their mind is too busy, or they find it nearly impossible 'not to think'. Meditation isn't about 'not thinking' or emptying your head of thoughts. This is the misconception I hear most often. It's about training your brain to focus its attention on one thing. People often say they can't do that, they find it impossible, but it comes with practice. It was a revelation for me to learn that the act of bringing your attention back to the thing you're focusing on (e.g. the breath) is the practice of meditation itself. Just like continually lifting a weight will build muscle in an arm, consistently bringing the attention back to the point of focus will build the ability to meditate. So when the mind wanders, the meditation isn't a failure. Our brain is like a wayward puppy, out of control. Catching it and putting it back to the object of focus *is* the mediation.

- Some people are afraid that by meditating they will lose their edge; their drive to succeed personally or professionally; they will be too calm, relaxed and brimming with peace to be effective in life. It's not about that at all. It's about understanding how your mind works – the thinking patterns you get caught up in – and then training your attention to be more focused when needed. This helps us to see situations more clearly and take wiser action.

- Finally, having been bombarded by magazine photos and YouTube clips of an archetypical meditation pose, people believe in order to meditate properly, they need to be sitting cross-legged on a cushion, palms of their hands facing the sky, wearing yoga pants, with a small column of meditation stones by their side. It's true some people do find it more comfortable to sit cross-legged on a cushion, and if that works for you, all well and good. However, many people meditate sitting on a chair, or standing up if need be. You can meditate on public transport and even when walking. There will be more advice on what do with your body when you meditate within the details of the specific exercises.

*

Calming the Mind Exercise 1:
Mindfulness Meditation

One of the most effective ways to start meditating is by focusing on something that is always with us – our breath. For this exercise just follow the instructions on the audio recording using the link further down the page.

I'd suggest you practise this meditation once a day, with the intention of doing it most days. You can do it using a posture that is comfortable for you, but you should aim to be alert and not sleepy. Feel free to use a chair, or sit on a cushion, but aim to adopt an erect and dignified posture if your environment allows you to. When I first started meditating I would often lie down on my bed or the floor, but I found myself falling asleep more often than not. You can choose any time of the day to do the meditation, whichever suits you best, many people find meditating first thing in the morning sets them up well for the rest of the day, but any time of the day will be beneficial.

You can find an audio recording of the guided meditation here: https://soundcloud.com/dr-matt-lewis

You can listen to it on your computer, phone, tablet, or MP3 player. Start with the 10 minute exercise, and then try some longer meditations when you feel ready. It's best to start with the shorter meditations to help you become confident with the practice, also making it easier to commit to it and build a habit. However, feel free to stick with the ten minute meditation if you feel ten minutes is about right for you.

As time goes by and you get used to the format of the meditation, you might feel like you don't need to use the recording. You will soon realise the process of meditation is quite simple and you will be able to fit it into your life more spontaneously – when you have the time and space to do so –

even if you're on public transport or sitting on a park bench. With a little experience you can design your own meditations to fit into any time frame, from as short as one minute upwards. The general structure of a mindfulness meditation is as follows:

- **Intention**: Start by creating an intention for your meditation. At the moment it may be to reduce your anxiety, lower your stress, or to be calmer throughout the day. Every time you create an intention you're forming or reinforcing a mental habit, and this action alone can start to guide your behaviour and positively impact on your decision making.

- **Follow your breath**: Just gently bring your attention to your breathing. People do this in many different ways; focusing on the feeling of the breath entering and leaving the nostrils, or becoming aware of the rising and falling of the chest.

- **Distraction**: You may find yourself in a state where your mind is calm and concentrated, gently following the breath, but sooner or later you will find yourself falling into distraction, worrying, or fantasising (much sooner rather than later when you first start meditating). This is normal. After a while you will notice your attention has wandered, and most people, especially beginners, react to this realisation with self-criticism, telling themselves they're terrible meditators. At this point you should:

- **Bring your attention back to the breath**: Remember, noticing your attention has wandered and then bringing it back to the breath is the process of the meditation itself. This is not a failure, it is what it is all about. So you should try to do this with kindness to yourself and with an attitude of curiosity.

If you enjoy walking, or as a part of your everyday routine you need to walk often, you may find it easier to do a walking meditation. It has the same focus and rigour as a sitting meditation, and can also help during anxious times, when the physiological reactions occurring in the body make it difficult to sit still. Don't worry, a walking meditation doesn't involve closing your eyes or any cushion carrying – it's about where and how you focus your attention when you're out and about.

Calming the Mind Exercise 2: Walking Meditation

Walking meditation is very simple, it involves bringing moment-to-moment attention to the movements of your walking, and every time your attention wanders away, bringing it back to those movements. To help you start, there is a guided walking meditation you can listen to as you walk here:

https://soundcloud.com/dr-matt-lewis/walking-meditation

If you find it difficult to carve out enough time for the formal sitting or walking meditation exercises, you can still incorporate mindfulness into other areas of your life, just as you're going about your everyday routines. Even if you *are* able to find time for the formal practices, you can extend their benefits by practising mindfulness in this way too. You can train yourself to focus your attention on whatever you are doing, whether it be walking, running, drawing, making a hot drink, or sitting down.

So in times when you would normally reach for your smartphone to waste a few moments, such as when you're waiting in queue; focus on your breath for a few moments instead. Of course, it wouldn't be beneficial or practical for you to do everything mindfully, but you can inject some mindfulness into your day by focusing intently on whatever you are doing and bringing your attention consistently back to the activity whenever your mind wanders.

Calming the Mind Exercise 3: Routine Tasks

This exercise is designed to help us to be awake for a few more moments each day, and not to be on autopilot when we are doing a routine every day activity. Choose one of the following activities, or one of your own choosing, and try to pay attention when you're doing it. You can choose different activities on different days or stick to one activity if you find it particularly helpful.

When you choose an activity, go at your own pace; you don't have to slow it down, or even enjoy it, but see if you can be fully alive and aware of your actions as you do it. When your attention wanders, as it will, just gently bring it back to the task: focusing carefully on all the actions and physical sensations of the task.

- Walking from one room to another

- Brushing your teeth

- Taking a shower

- Getting dressed or undressed

- Making the bed

- Making breakfast

- Drinking tea, coffee, water, or juice

- Doing the dishes or filling the dishwasher

- Taking out the rubbish (trash)

- Loading the washing machine or tumble drier

- Waiting in a queue (look at people and objects around you, listen to the different sounds etc.)

- Waiting at traffic lights (whilst still being aware of the colour of the lights, notice the sights and sounds around you).

*

Calming the Mind Exercise 4:
The Power Pose

Recent research by Harvard psychologist Amy Cuddy has demonstrated that standing for two minutes in a 'power pose' – a stance in which we expand our body and take up space – has the benefit of increasing testosterone (a hormone that makes us feel powerful) and decreasing cortisol (a hormone released during the fight, flight, or freeze response that makes us feel anxious).[28] When we are anxious, we tend to physically retreat with our body, drawing our arms and legs inward and hunching over, but when we expand our body we can drive a change in hormonal chemistry that can help lift anxiety and allow us access to our best thinking.

Amy Cuddy's TED talk explaining the research can be found here:
https://www.ted.com/speakers/amy_cuddy

I would also recommend Cuddy's book: *Presence: Bringing Your Boldest Self to Your Biggest Challenges'* for detailed information and research on the power of body language.

Doing this exercise in the morning when you get up can make a substantial difference to how you approach the day ahead (honestly, just try it).

Also use this exercise when you're feeling panicked, anxious, stressed, or facing a challenging situation. The research suggests it's particularly helpful before situations in which we're being socially evaluated, such as job interviews, or presentations. The original studies demonstrated that people who did a two minute power pose before an important interview performed better than those who were in neutral or 'low power' poses – these are closed stances and guarded body language.

Examples of a power pose are:

Wonder Woman – Standing with your feet slightly apart, hands on your hips, chest out, and chin up (think of the pose 'Wonder Woman' is famous for).

The Victor – Stand as if you have just won the Olympic 100 metres sprint. Legs apart, arms aloft in a 'V' shape, chest out, and chin up.

The Villain – Sit back in a chair with your feet resting on an object in front of you, such as a desk or table, with your hands resting behind your head.

The CEO – Lean slightly over a flat waist-high surface, such as a desk or table, with your hands wide apart resting on the surface.

The Subway Guy – Sit in a chair and spread out your body, legs apart and arms stretched out at the sides.

You can find pictorial examples of these poses at: www.drmattlewis.com/power-poses/

Step 2:
Dealing with Anxious Thoughts and Feelings

Chapter 7
Defusion: Managing Anxious Thoughts

We discussed the ACT mindfulness skills of defusion, expansion, and engagement, earlier on in Chapter 3, explaining they can help us to manage our anxious thinking. This section of the book includes three short chapters, one on each of these ACT skills. The best way to understand and learn these skills is to try them out for yourself. While they may seem a little contrived at first, after some practice they become easy to implement, and after a short while you will find you are able to do them intuitively and with very little effort.

In Chapter 3 we also discussed the pathways to anxiety, and said our cortex can initiate anxiety in one of two ways:

- by interpreting neutral sensory information as dangerous, and sending this information to the amygdala to produce anxiety;

- or by independently creating anxious thoughts and feelings, without sensory information, and again, sending this information to the amygdala to produce anxiety.

With practice, we can learn to manage these unhelpful thoughts, and stop, or at least greatly reduce, the reaction of the amygdala, allowing us to take control of our behaviour and engage fully with our actions. We're now going to learn how to put the skills into practice that will allow us to do this, focusing firstly on defusion.

MANAGING OUR THOUGHTS

At the heart of defusion are words and images. We use words in different contexts:

- Words we read are called text.
- Words we speak out loud are called speech.
- Words inside our head are called thoughts.

The thoughts inside our head can also be images; still images like photographs, or moving images like film clips. We often forget our thoughts are just words or images that we often turn into stories. These stories can be true (facts) or false (lies), but they are normally based on how we see life; through our experiences, opinions, judgements and morals; and are about what we have done in the past, or what we want, expect, or fear in the future.

I want to make it clear - thinking is important - this book is not against thinking! Thinking allows us to learn from the past and plan for the future. These are key human skills we need to survive and thrive, but sometimes we can get too caught up in our thoughts and stories, and when they are unhelpful, this can lead to difficulties. An unhelpful thought or story can dominate our mind, take up our full attention, and dictate our behaviour. This is called 'fusion' – the act of getting caught up in our thoughts and considering them to be absolutely true.

To counteract unhelpful thoughts and stories we can defuse, or separate, from them — become aware they are just thoughts. When we defuse from our thoughts, we are putting the brakes on unhelpful thinking. We are creating a small gap of awareness that allows us to stop or greatly reduce the anxious thoughts and the resultant anxiety response.

There are a number of ways we can defuse from our thoughts, and in time and with practice, it is something we can learn to do almost automatically when needed. I'd recommend you try all of the following defusion exercises and see which ones work best for you.

This first exercise is to illustrate how defusion works, but it can also be used as a practice to defuse from unhelpful thoughts and stories.

Defusion Exercise 1: I Notice I'm Having the Thought

Step 1
Bring to mind a negative thought about yourself, one you have often. Maybe it's, "*I'm a loser*', '*No one likes me*', or '*I'll fail*'. Thought of one?

Step 2
Now 'Fuse' with that thought. That is, believe it as much as you can.

Step 3
Now insert this phrase in front of that thought…"<u>I'm having the thought that…</u>"
For example, 'I'm having the thought that…I'm a loser.'

Step 4
Next insert an extra phrase in front of that phrase…"<u>I notice that</u> I'm having the thought that…"
For example, 'I notice that I'm having the thought that…I'm a loser.'

Can you feel the thought lose some of its impact?

You'll notice in this exercise you weren't battling or disputing the thought, you were accepting it, but not letting it influence you. When we defuse from our thoughts like this, we start to realise thoughts are nothing more or less than words or pictures and we can let them chatter away without obeying them. Negative thoughts are normal, so don't fight them, defuse from them.

The second defusion technique targets the power of stories. The mind loves stories, but unfortunately many of them are unhelpful and negative, such as 'I can't do it', 'My life is terrible', 'I'll fail'. In fact, research shows about eighty per cent of our thoughts have some negative content, but negative stories aren't the problem, the problem is getting caught up in them and letting them dictate our actions.

When our mind tells us an unhelpful story, we normally try to **change it** ('No I'm not stupid, I'm capable, I've done this, this and this'), **distract ourselves from it**, or **blank it out** in some way. Trying to change, avoid, or get rid of that story is often ineffective, time consuming, and focuses our attention on the unhelpful story. Instead, simply name a story for what it is – a story.

As a personal example, when considering doing things outside of my comfort zone, my mind would often respond with, 'Don't be stupid. You stupid idiot Matthew.' When I learned about defusion, I called that 'The Matthew is Stupid' story. Stories start to lose their impact when we start naming them – then we begin to realise they are just stories.

Defusion Exercise 2: The Power of Stories

Step 1
Notice when your mind starts telling you a familiar story. It may not always use the exact same thoughts or images each time, but there will be a pattern of thinking or a narrative you recognise.

Step 2

Name the story (silently in your head) *Ah! There it is again the – 'I'm a Loser' story, 'I'm fat' story, 'I can't cope' story, 'I'm unlovable' story, 'Not good enough' story.* Give it any name you want.

Step 3

Continue to name the story every time you notice it, but try to do it with warmth, and if appropriate, humour.

So when an unhelpful thought or story comes, we need to notice it, name it, and neutralise it. Although this may seem like a very simple strategy, you are training your cortex to be aware of your sticky thoughts and thinking patterns, and in time you will start to see the stories will lose their impact on your behaviour.

*

Defusion Exercise 3: Thanking the Mind

The third defusion technique is simple, quick, and effective, and it's the one I personally find most helpful. When your mind comes up with those same old stories or unhelpful thoughts, simply thank it.

Say (silently to yourself), *'Thanks mind!'*, *'Thanks for sharing!'*, *'Is that right?'*, *'That's amazing!'*, *'That's so informative!'* Don't do this sarcastically or aggressively, but do it with warmth, humour, and genuine appreciation for the incredible storytelling ability of your mind. This simple act of noticing and acknowledging the thoughts or stories will start to reduce their power.

Some people find it helpful to give their mind a name when they thank it, and find the name creates a slighter larger gap of awareness. For example, *'Thanks for the thought George, thanks for sharing!'*

IMAGES AND MOVING PICTURES

If your unhelpful thoughts are appearing in the form of images, or video style film clips, of memories and predictions of what could happen, there are a number of different strategies you can use to defuse from them. The strategies are very similar to the previous ones, in that they provide a gap of awareness that allows you to step back and observe your thoughts before taking action.

Defusion Exercise 4: Lights, Camera, Action!

Step 1

When you have an unhelpful image or video clip pop into your head, imagine there's a television near you, and put the image or video on the television

Step 2

Now play around with the image. Turn it upside down, flip it around, stretch it, play the video backwards, turn the colour and brightness up and down. There are lots of ways you can play with it; give it subtitles, a soundtrack, or put it in different locations. It doesn't have to be a television – you can put the image on a computer screen, poster, or t-shirt – be creative and see what works best for you.

Remember, the aim isn't to get rid of unpleasant images, but to see them for what they are – just pictures.

HELP WITH DEFUSION

Try out some of these exercises when you're having unhelpful thoughts or imagining unpleasant images and see which ones work best for you. Don't expect miraculous overnight changes – although this is possible – it normally takes some practice, but you will start to see progress sooner rather than later.

When you first start to practise defusion, just notice your experience without judging yourself; rather than being critical, be curious about it. With persistence you will eventually notice being aware of unhelpful thoughts and defusing from them becomes second nature, and in time you'll be able to do it without using any techniques.

WHAT IF MY THOUGHTS ARE TRUE?

When first hearing about defusion, people often respond by asking *'But what if the thoughts are true?'* The thought or thoughts you are having may well be true, but a more important question is: *'Are my thoughts helpful?'*

So for example, when trying to do something new, something you may find difficult, you may have the thought, *'I'm incompetent, I'll never be able to do this'*. It may be true that you do not have the skills to do that particular task properly at that time, but does holding that thought encourage you to look after yourself or to take action? For some people it might, they may find that sort of thought motivates them. If it does, that's fine. Fuse with it. However, most people would find a thought like that blaming and demoralising, and it doesn't encourage them to look after themselves or to take action. It would be unhelpful.

An example of a more helpful thought that could come, one that may be better to fuse with, or hold on to, is 'I can ask for help" or 'With practice I will get better'. Most people would consider that to be an encouraging thought, one that could lead to helpful behaviour. Remember you're not replacing one thought with another, you're noticing what is an unhelpful thought and what is a helpful thought, and deciding whether to hold onto and fuse with that thought, or to defuse from it. So what's important is not whether or not a thought is true, but whether or not holding onto that thought helps you to take care of yourself and take positive action.

*

THE MAIN PURPOSE OF DEFUSION

People often get the wrong idea about defusion, thinking it's a clever way to get rid of negative thoughts. This is because, often when we defuse from a thought, it disappears and over time shows up less. However, think of this as a lucky bonus, a by-product of defusion. It may not always happen and is not the main purpose of defusion. The main purpose of defusion is to be present and to be able to take effective action. Defusion isn't about battling with, blocking, distracting from, or getting rid of thoughts, but accepting thoughts and defusing from them.

*

Now we've learned how to handle thoughts and images, in the next chapter we're going to explain how we deal with unpleasant and uncomfortable feelings.

Chapter 8
Expansion: Managing Anxious Feelings

When we experience painful or uncomfortable feelings, emotions, or sensations, we normally do our best to avoid them, distract ourselves from them, or try to get rid of them. When we do this we can often find relief in the short-term, but make our lives more difficult in the long-term. We can learn to deal with these feelings effectively by learning a skill called 'expansion'.

In ACT the term 'expansion' is really another name for **acceptance**. We're using the term *expansion* as most people misunderstand acceptance to mean wanting, tolerating, liking, or putting up with. In the context of ACT, this is not the case.

Expansion can be described as the ability to open up and make room for emotions, sensations, and feelings. Allowing them to come and go without letting them drag us down, push us around, or hold us back. It's a powerful way to handle difficult emotions such as fear, anger and anxiety.

So rather than trying to get rid of unpleasant feelings, we open up and accommodate them. We make room and allow them to come and go in their own good time. It doesn't mean we want them, like them, or approve of them, but we just stop investing our time and effort in fighting them. The more space we can give difficult feelings, the smaller their influence and impact on our lives.

The following exercise illustrates how expansion works, but it can also be used to practise expansion when you're experiencing uncomfortable emotions, feelings, or sensations.

Expansion Exercise: N.A.M.E
(Notice, Acknowledge, Make Space, Expand Awareness)

Step 1
Think of something that makes you mildly anxious. Nothing too extreme, just something that gives you some mild to moderate anxious feelings, whether it's driving in heavy traffic, having to order something at a busy bar (one of mine), or walking into a room of strangers. Maybe it's an up-and-coming task you have to do you're not looking forward to. Take a little time to think of something.

Step 2
Observe. Now observe the sensations in your body. Just thinking about that situation should bring about some feelings in your body. Just observe those sensations. Where are they in your body? There maybe more than one sensation, if so, look for the one that bothers you the most. Be curious about it. Where does it start and stop? What shape do you imagine it to be? Is it light or heavy? Is it moving or staying still? Is it warm or cool?

Step 3
Breathe. Now breathe into and around the sensation. Slow, deep breaths if you can. Deep breaths can lower the tension in your body, increase your vagal tone, and help you to switch from the sympathetic nervous system (fight or flight, and aggressive) to the parasympathetic nervous system (calmer and restful). This won't get rid of your feelings but it will provide some calmness within you. Like an anchor in the storm. Imagine your breath

flowing into and around the sensation.

Step 4

Make space. As your breath flows in and around the sensation, imagine it's creating extra space within your body, so you're giving it plenty of room to move. If the feeling gets bigger, give it even more space, allow it even more room.

Step 5

Allow. Now allow that sensation to be there, even though you may not like it or want it. Just let it be there. If your mind comments on what's happening, just thank it and go back to observing. You may feel an urge to fight it or push it away, if so, just acknowledge that urge and bring your attention back to the sensation or feeling. Remember you're not trying to get rid of it or change it, but if it changes by itself that's fine. Keep observing it until you completely give up the struggle with it and accept it.

Step 6

Expand awareness. When you've given up the struggle with the sensation, expand your awareness to the present moment, whatever is happening right now. What is happening in the room you're in? What can you see, hear, smell? Think of it as being like bringing the lights up on a stage. Normally when we're anxious we have a spotlight focusing only on the anxious feeling. Now however, you've acknowledged the sensation and you're bringing up the lights and taking in your environment.

This should give you a taste of what expansion is like. At times you may experience lots of sensations, and if this is the case, go through one after the other, using the technique until you stop struggling. With practice you'll learn to do this naturally and quickly – you'll notice an uncomfortable emotion or feeling, and rather than trying to control it, or allow it to control you,

you'll accept it and give it space, allowing it to come and go while being able to engage in the present moment.

Take the example a job interview. Just before going into the room you may start to feel very anxious. This is perfectly normal. Rather than leaving the situation or arguing with your feelings, you can notice the anxiety, give it space, and allow it to come and go, while 'bringing up the lights' on your environment. This will allow you to engage with the present moment – the people in the room and questions you're being asked. The anxiety may still be there, but it is not controlling your behaviour.

Like defusion, people often get the wrong idea about expansion – that it's a clever way to get rid of uncomfortable or painful feelings – as when we use expansion, the uncomfortable feeling often disappears and over time shows up less. However, don't expect this each time, consider it a lucky bonus, a by-product of expansion and not the main purpose. The main aim of expansion is to reduce the influence and impact of the difficult feelings in order for us to be able to present and take effective action.

Chapter 9
Engagement

So far in this section we've talked about defusion: accepting unhelpful thoughts but reducing or eliminating their impact on us; followed by expansion: accepting uncomfortable feelings, letting them come and go, but not allowing them to influence us. The next step is engaging with experiences, tasks, and situations, despite unhelpful thoughts and uncomfortable feelings — staying present and engaging with life.

Engagement is the ability to be present instead of caught up in our thoughts. It is about being fully in the moment; being open to, curious about, and actively involved in our here and now experience. Being able to be engaged and present is essential if we need to perform well in challenging situations or if we want to find satisfaction and fulfilment in whatever we are doing.

If we want to do anything well; learn a difficult skill, play a musical instrument, perform well at an interview, or talk to strangers; we need to be engaged in what is happening. Being anxious or having negative thoughts about doing something is not the problem. The problem is being caught up and lost in these thoughts and being disengaged from our experience. The more we focus on the unhelpful thoughts and feelings, the more we disconnect from the present moment. If we are continually inside our head, we're paralysed, unable to take action, or if we do take action, it's in a distracted and less effective way.

This particularly tends to happen when we experience anxiety. We get hooked on stories about the future, about how things might go wrong and how badly we'll handle them. This stops us from taking action and makes us even more anxious in the long run, it's a vicious circle. If a person feels lonely because they are anxious about socialising with others, they may often choose to stay at home instead of going out to meet with friends. This may relieve their anxiety, but just makes the situation worse over time – they become lonelier. In order to live life fully we need to begin to practise engaging with the present moment despite feeling anxious.

We don't have to be connected to the present moment all the time. It's fine to be lost in our thoughts sometimes. However, it is particularly useful to be present in a number of situations. Such as in activities we find pleasant – that nourish us – it's beneficial to be fully engaged in these activities and not lost in anxiety or worry. Likewise, there are some activities, tasks, or situations that we may not find pleasant – taking an exam, going to a medical appointment, completing a difficult project – but we need to engage with them in order to get what we want out of life, to protect ourselves, and to open doors to opportunities me might otherwise miss. Practising engagement allows us to be fully present when we really need to.

Engagement, or fully paying attention to something, is also a clever way to silence negative thoughts as it deliberately overloads our attentional bandwidth. For example, when feeling anger, we can focus our attention on something in such a way that anger isn't an option. Try ranting while also engrossed in a crossword puzzle, it's impossible. You can also do the same with anxiety. The key is to pause, be aware of the stories going on inside your head, use defusion, allow any uncomfortable feelings to come and go in their own time, and then engage or focus fully on the task in hand.

*

Let's go through some exercises that will allow us to practise engagement. Then, when we we're feeling anxious and really do need to engage with a task, activity, or situation, we will have the ability to focus our attention on our environment and the present moment. Increasing our ability to focus our attention is a skill that can be learned, and the more we practise, the easier we will find it.

Engagement Exercise: Engaging with Activities

Engaging with a Neutral Activity

In the *'Calming the Mind'* chapter we introduced an exercise that encouraged staying present when completing routine tasks (Exercise 3), so this should have given you a taste of practising engaging with the present moment while doing a neutral task. Pick a task or activity you feel neutral about (you find it neither pleasant or unpleasant) and engage with it fully, focusing carefully on all the actions and physical sensations of the task. If your mind starts to wander, bring your attention back to the activity and be fully present with what you are doing.

Engaging with a Pleasant Activity

Now practise engagement — being fully present — when doing a pleasant activity. This should be something you enjoy, so will differ from individual to individual; it may involve eating a nice lunch, walking your dog, reading a book, doing a sudoku puzzle, listening to birds, sitting in the sunshine, having a hug. You decide. Connect or engage with the task fully, through the five senses, defusing your thoughts and making room for your feelings. If your mind starts to wander, bring your attention back fully to the task.

Engaging with a Task You Have Been Avoiding

Using the same principles as above, stay present when doing an activity or task you have been avoiding. Something you may have been putting off for a while. Maybe because it's an unpleasant, boring, or disagreeable activity. Connect or engage with the task fully through the fives senses, defusing your thoughts and making room for your feelings. If your mind starts to wander, bring your attention back fully to the task.

It's important to note we don't have to be present or engaged with absolutely everything we do, all the time. These are just exercises to help us practise being engaged with the present moment – whether it's neutral, pleasant, or unpleasant – so we can do so when we really need to.

Sometimes it may be beneficial to think of something else when we're doing an activity or task. It's fine to plan what we're going to do with our evening when we're washing the dishes or cleaning the floor. The problem is when our anxious feelings drive unhelpful behaviour; when we are avoiding activities we need to do, perform poorly at a task we want to do well in, or are not benefitting from being present in a pleasurable activity that will nourish us.

*

In the next section we're going to combine the skills we have learned so far and apply them in a practical way. We'll use them to overcome fear, to take action when it really matters, and to be confident at doing anything.

Step 3:
Taking Action

Chapter 10
Overcoming Fear

We tend to use the terms 'anxiety' and 'fear' interchangeably, but while anxiety is normally to do with worrying about possible *events before they occur*, fear can be defined as our psychological reaction to *events that are happening*. So anxiety is concerned with the future, often causing us to avoid situations, or stopping us from starting tasks or activities. Fear, on the other hand, is a reaction to what is happening in the present, and can cause us to stop what we're doing or to underperform.

Fear is important and appropriate in many situations and is there for our protection; if a car is hurtling towards us at high speed, it's appropriate to feel fear and get out of the way as quickly as possible. However, we can also feel fear in situations when it isn't helpful, and it can stop us from stepping outside of our comfort zone.

When we are experiencing an event that causes fear to rise within us, we find it unpleasant and often try to withdraw, block, or distract ourselves from it. Sometimes these strategies work because we are in real danger and may need to flee or fight. It's also reasonable to withdraw from a situation, or avoid it altogether, if the fear doesn't present much of a problem or has little consequence for us. If riding large roller coasters overwhelms you with fear, it won't hold you back in life if you never bother to ride them. If you are afraid of public speaking, but have no desire to speak in public and are never required to do so, then the fear won't impact on your life.

However, when fear is holding us back from doing something we really value or want to do; or causes us extreme distress and arises frequently; then we need to work on tackling and overcoming it. We need to learn to tolerate our fear and become comfortable with feeling discomfort.

Tolerating Discomfort

When I was in my twenties, I helped a friend who owned a construction company by labouring for him on a building project. We had two weeks to demolish and rebuild some outside buildings for a supermarket. Most of my work involved demolishing walls, carrying bricks, clearing away rubbish, and mixing cement. On one particular Sunday morning, when the site was empty, I was due to work on one outside area on my own. It started pouring down with rain just as I arrived at the building site in the morning and it didn't stop all day long. Regardless of the weather, the job had to be done.

Normally we try as much as possible to shelter ourselves from the rain, and if we do go out in it, we tend to cover ourselves with an umbrella or wear waterproofs. On this occasion I was left on the building site with a job that had to be finished, with no shelter from the rain, and no waterproofs to put on. For the first ten minutes I grumbled and complained to myself; my face was stinging from the hard, heavy rain, and my clothes got soaking wet as I carried brick after brick from the demolished building to a skip.

However, after a while I got used to the rain and it stopped bothering me. My inner complaining dialogue almost completely stopped and I got into a rhythm of working. I noticed how the raindrops felt softer when falling onto my arms than they did when they hit my face, and how the rain felt as it dripped from my hair, down my face, onto my neck, and settled at the top of the collar of my t-shirt. When I got used to the wet clothes sticking to my skin, that felt fine too. I noticed how the wet material of my t-shirt felt differently to that of my jeans against my skin. I had no choice but to stay there and get used to the discomfort, with no means of avoidance or distraction.

When I first arrived I'd had a sense of dread and self-pity when I noticed the rain starting to pour. However, as time passed and I mindfully noticed the present moment sensations of the rain, I discovered it was nowhere near as bad as I had initially expected. What I didn't know at the time was I'd defused from my thoughts, accepted the discomfort, and engaged with the present moment. I can't say I enjoyed it, but I did get the job done.

Suppose you could defuse from thoughts about how bad or unpleasant your fear is and how much you dislike it. If instead of trying to make it go away, you non-judgmentally notice the physical sensations and then focus your attention on engaging with what you are doing? Trying to get rid of fear and anxiety takes up a lot of energy and is very distracting. It's like constantly wiping rain away from your face and pulling your wet clothes away from your skin. It's hard to engage in life when you're busy arguing with your thoughts and struggling with your feelings.

The Illusions of Fear

We often think that before we are able to do anything properly, we have to get rid of the fear of doing it. We believe we simply can't function well when we are experiencing fear. However, there are a number of illusions surrounding fear that begin to fade away when we look at them a little more closely.

- **Fear is a weakness**: when we step out of our comfort zone we will experience fear. It's natural and normal. There's no way of expanding your comfort zone without stepping outside of it and feeling fear. Fear is not a sign of weakness, it is a sign we are pushing our boundaries and progressing.

- **Fear is debilitating**: when we leave our comfort zone and 'put ourselves out there', especially into public arena, we are taking a risk. This can trip our fight, flight, or freeze response, along with many of the physiological reactions we have already talked about. In most cases it's unavoidable, and we need to accept this. Sporting or artistic performers sometimes refer to this fear as being 'psyched up', 'pumped', or 'wired'. In many situations we can learn to channel our fear and use it to good effect, increasing the level of our performance. More often than not, the fear won't debilitate us, but focusing on the fear will.

- **Fear will keep us stuck**: when we hold on to the attitude that fear is bad and we can't do anything until it goes away, it will keep us stuck. When facing challenges, some people use drugs to numb the fear; cancel or avoid appointments, performances, and tasks; or even stop doing things altogether, especially after a bad experience. However, this will often make things worse in the long-term. Fear doesn't hold us back, but our attitude to fear does.

Managing Fear

Knowing the illusions surrounding fear is all well and good, but when we're in a real-life challenging situation that doesn't require us to fight, flee, or freeze, what can we practically do when we feel fear rising up?

1. Firstly, we need to accept it. We can't numb, push away, or eliminate fear when it arises. Battling or arguing with it will only take our attention away from the situation or task in hand, meaning we'll be unable to be present and do whatever we need to as well as we possibly can. When I first started university lecturing, I was terrified, and would often spend much of the lecture caught up in my fear; criticising myself for feeling so afraid, wondering what the students were thinking about my shaky voice and trembling hands, slowly becoming convinced I didn't have what it took to do the job properly. It was only after I accepted the fear and focused on my lecture material that my performances improved and I became more confident. I still often feel fear when lecturing, but I've learned to accept it and focus on the task in hand.

2. It can also help if we take a step further than just accepting fear when it arises, and purposely welcome it. *Hello fear my old friend.* That's not to say we go out looking for fear, or we like it's presence, but when we do notice it we aren't harsh or bitter, instead we're warm and welcoming to it. We need to be aware fear evolved to help keep us safe in challenging situations, to alert us to risks, and to prime us for action. It means well and is on our side. We can build a positive relationship with fear, win its trust, and discover it's harmless. While this may sound ridiculous, it will allow us to see fear for what it is and to work at being confident in those situations and tasks we want, or need to do. So accept it and welcome it.

3. Finally, we can use it. When we feel fear and our sympathetic nervous system initiates the emergency or challenge response, our senses get heightened, our reflexes quicken, we get greater strength, and our body is energised and ready for action. Sometimes we can use this extra energy and focus to our advantage. It can be particularly helpful for physical tasks or activities.

We may also benefit from changing the way we interpret the symptoms of fear. We talked about how important mindset is in the Introduction. Adding to that evidence is some new research suggesting that if we interpret our fear as 'excitement', we're more likely to use it to take action that will result in more positive behaviour. This is because excitement, like fear, is a high arousal state. Eliminating a high arousal state is almost impossible, but reinterpreting it is relatively easy. The research demonstrated that reframing fear as excitement increased performance in a number of tasks, particularly those involving social evaluation.[29] So accept fear, welcome it as a friend, and when possible, use it to your benefit.

There will of course be situations in which we can't use the energy fear provides, like when we sit down to take an exam, or have to talk to our manager at work. So if you're in a situation in which you can't use your fear, just make room for it and then focus on engaging in the present moment and the task at hand.

*

So fear and anxiety shouldn't stop us from doing anything we want, or need to do. We can use the same principles to become confident at doing almost anything, even the things we currently don't have the skills or experience to do. We'll look at how this is possible in the next chapter.

Chapter 11
How to Be Confident at Doing Anything

As a university lecturer I was responsible for the personal guidance of a large number of students. Many of them would come to talk to me about their hopes and fears, and as I mentioned at the beginning of the book, quite a few of them shared their personal struggles with anxiety with me. However, there was always one type of task that seemed to strike fear into nearly all students, even the most capable and seemingly confident ones – the dreaded class presentation. Any task or assessment that involved standing up in front of the class and presenting, be it as individual or as part of a group, caused high levels of panic amongst many in the class.

I'm Just Not a Confident Person

A phrase I would often hear when students talked to me individually was *'I'm just not a very confident person.'* Many people tend to say this when faced with a situation or task they are uncomfortable about, but people forget there are many things they are very confident at doing, but take this confidence for granted.

To help students get over the belief they're not very

confident people, I would ask them to write a list of skills or tasks they were confident at doing, however simple. Sometimes they would stare at the blank piece of paper and say they couldn't think of anything. So I'd ask them if they were confident at walking. If so, they had to put it down on the list. Then I'd name more skills, such as eating, driving, catching a ball, climbing a ladder, handwriting, gaming, etc. Then we'd go through their list and I'd explain they weren't always confident at doing these things, but because they'd done them so many times, they take them for granted. So a universal or general lack of confidence isn't normally the issue; we tend to lack confidence in specific activities and certain areas of life.

WHY DO WE LACK SPECIFIC CONFIDENCE?

There are a number of reasons that lie behind our anxiety about trying something new or tackling something uncomfortable. We normally lack the confidence in our ability to do something due to one or a combination of the following:

- **We lack the expertise or skills required**: If we haven't got the skills to do something it wouldn't be natural to feel confident about doing it. I've never ridden a motorcycle before, so do you think it would be reasonable of me to feel confident about riding one?

- **We lack experience**: If we have little or no experience of doing something, then we can't expect to be confident about it. You may be able to sing well, but if you've never sung in front of a huge audience before, you're not likely to feel confident about doing it.

- **We have unreasonable aspirations**: We often have unreasonable expectations that are difficult to fulfill if we are trying something new, or have to do it in a challenging situation. We all get caught up in this type of perfectionism at times, that we shouldn't do it unless we are excellent at it, or at least extremely competent. This often stops us from doing something before we've even tried.

- **We engage in extreme self-criticism**: The human mind has a natural tendency to judge itself harshly: to criticise, to look for the negative, and predict the worst. This is just a normal human mind at work – the troublesome brain we discussed in the first section. It reminds us of negative stories from the past, creates gloomy future forecasts, and puts us off trying something before we've even started. It keeps us focused on what's wrong with us, makes us afraid of failure, and causes us to give up more easily. It makes us less resilient in the face of challenges and therefore less likely to learn from mistakes.

- **We focus on fear**: We may be afraid of failing, of being embarrassed, of rejection, of others laughing at us, or of fear itself. However, as we discussed earlier, fear in itself does not affect our performance, but focusing on the fear does. The more we focus on our fear the more it is likely to undermine our confidence.

The Confidence Cycle

So how do we overcome all of these barriers, build confidence, and become good at doing something? Well there are no magic bullets and no shortcuts; a hypnotic trance won't help us, and neither will attending a weekend 'Super Confidence' workshop. Sure, we can psych ourselves up and feel good about doing something for a short while, but the effect won't last long, especially when we step outside of our comfort zone and into the real world.

However, the good news is we can feel confident about, and be good at, doing almost anything. We've done it countless times before – when we learned to walk, talk, eat, tell the time – all the way through to operating a computer and driving a car. We're going to follow the same process now, using what is called in ACT, The Confidence Cycle.

Dr. Russ Harris, a world-renowned ACT trainer, outlines the four steps of the confidence cycle in his book *The Confidence Gap*.[30] I've always considered a more appropriate name for the process could be 'The Learning Cycle', because it's a process for learning news skills and teaching yourself to be able to perform them in challenging situations. It is only after we are able to do this we can truly feel confident.

The Confidence Cycle is also a reminder of how important a growth mindset is. We become good at something, and confident at doing it, by practising it, and not because we were born with a special gift or disposition. Our abilities and skills aren't fixed – we become experts in, or competent at, the things we practise.

The Confidence Cycle

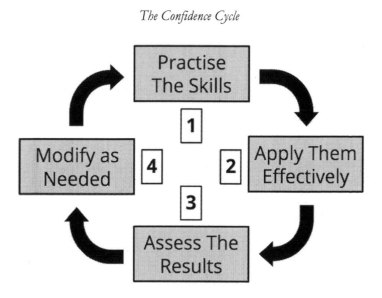

1. PRACTISE THE SKILLS

If we want to get good at anything and feel confident about it, we need to practise – whether it's public speaking, painting, or playing the guitar. Keeping this in mind helps us to overcome the mental barriers to practice – the things that stop us from starting to learn, or force us to give up relatively quickly. These mental barriers include: feeling anxious or fearful, the desire to give up when progress is slow, the tendency to quit after an initial failure, perfectionism, or extreme self-criticism. So whenever you're practising a new skill and come up against one of those mental barriers, accept what you're feeling is normal, but understand persevering will help you to get past that barrier and on the road to confidently performing a new skill.

2. APPLY THEM EFFECTIVELY

Practising the skills is important, and it's the place we must start at, but we need to do more than that if we want to feel confident about doing something well. We also need to step out of our comfort zone and apply our practised skills effectively – into real life challenging situations.

After putting their presentations together and practising in their own rooms, I always used to give my students the opportunity to practise in front of other students in purposely arranged sessions. Those who practised in front of others nearly always performed better in the real presentation assessment. As we've learned, leaving our comfort zone makes us feel uncomfortable, so we need to practise our skills in real life uncomfortable situations. By doing this we can learn to focus on what we are doing rather than getting caught up in our thoughts and feelings. This is called *Task Focused Attention*; and applying the mindfulness skills we've outlined in the previous chapters – defusion, expansion, and engagement – will help us to do this. We need to think of uncomfortable and challenging situations as an opportunity to learn.

*

3. ASSESS THE RESULTS

After applying our skills in a challenging situation, rather than burying our heads in the sand, we need to reflect on the results. We need to consider what did and didn't work, and what could we do differently the next time to improve our performance. There are some key points we need to keep in mind when reflecting on our performance:

- Firstly, it's important we reflect in a non-judgemental way, and remember we are in the process of learning. So we should avoid being extremely self-critical. Harsh self-judgement is rarely helpful and often pushes us in the direction of quitting; discouraging us from learning further. When we were toddlers learning to walk, if we stumbled and fell, we didn't think *'Well, I'm not doing that again, I felt like a right idiot! I'll never be able to walk properly.'* So when you assess the results, always keep in mind that learning is a process, and be compassionate and encouraging in your self-reflection. Self-compassion increases motivation and willpower, brings greater perspective, and boosts decision making. This all makes us more resilient – making it easier to bounce back in the face of failure and learn from mistakes.

- Secondly, avoid comparing yourself to others, especially when assessing your results. It's helpful to have an expert training or teaching you, someone with a higher skill level, but look only at how you can improve against your own performance. If you do start comparing yourself to others, use the defusion, expansion, and engagement skills, and focus compassionately on your own results. It's fine to aspire to those who perform the activity better than you, but too much emphasis on the performance of others during the learning stage can have a negative impact on motivation.

*

4. MODIFY AS NEEDED

The next step is to modify what you are doing. Do more of what is working well and change or modify what isn't going well. During the presentation practice sessions I arranged at the university, I would instruct the students in my class to write down a list of what went well and what didn't go so well, and how they could improve. It's the only way to develop and get better. As Einstein famously said, *"Insanity is doing the same thing over and over again and expecting different results."*

After you have modified what you are doing, you repeat the cycle until you get good at what you're trying to learn. Confidence will follow. The actions of confidence come first, the feelings of confidence come second.

Visualisation

Before introducing visualisation, I want to make it clear that when attempting to overcome anxiety and build confidence in specific activities, tasks, or areas of life, *there is no substitute for real life practice*. However, visualisation can be a very powerful additional tool when used correctly.

Visualisation is sometimes called imagery, mental rehearsal, or mental practice, and it refers to the creating or recreating of an experience in the mind. The process involves constructing or recalling from memory, pieces of information stored from experience, and shaping these pieces into meaningful images. It is like playing a film in your mind of a goal, activity, or task you intend to undertake. As an example, a tennis player might use visualisation by mentally rehearsing their serve in detail before playing match, or visualising a previously effective and winning performance before going on court.

MRI scans have indicated the brain doesn't distinguish between an imagined and an actual experience, so preparing for a challenge using visualisation can be a very useful tool to use before stepping out and practising learned skills in the real world. Let's look more closely at how visualisation can be used in conjunction with the confidence cycle.

Visualising future success: Visualising what success looks like can motivate us to start and continue the work of practising skills. Imagining a successful end goal can keep us in touch with our values, while also helping to keep us motivated when problems arise, things get difficult, or life is uncomfortable. It can also be a tool to keep us focused on where we are heading and why, clarifying our objectives.

When I went through difficulties during the writing of my PhD thesis, I often visualised what completing the PhD would look like for me, the career opportunities it would bring, and the security it would provide for my family. I'd try to picture how that would look and feel. In particularly uncomfortable times I would visualise myself on the stage at graduation, shaking the hand of the vice-chancellor as I received my certificate, and I'd imagine my completed and bound PhD thesis on a shelf in my office.

Visualising challenges: Mentally imagining the step-by-step process of a challenging future task or activity has a number of benefits. As we said, the brain can't tell the difference between a real and imagined experience, so going through a challenging task in detail can be excellent preparation.

Welsh rugby union player Leigh Halfpenny would often prepare for his goal-kicking by spending time visualising the process in his hotel room before the game; imagining the crowd, the tension, various kicking distances and angles, going through every single motion he would do for a real kick.[31] I would often do the same before important talks or lectures I had to deliver (not as glamorous as kicking the winning points for Wales, I know). If possible, I would go to the actual room of the talk some hours, days, or weeks beforehand so I could see the exact environment, and I'd imagine how it would feel full of people. If I didn't have access to the room or hall, I'd try to find photos of it online. Often before interviews or talks I'd check how the street and building looked on Google Maps, and imagine walking into the building in preparation.

Visualising challenges in this way can also prepare us for mistakes, or things going wrong. The Olympic record holding swimmer, Michael Phelps, often visualised his goggles filling with water, a competitor doing better than expected, or losing count of his strokes, and would then go through the process of how he would react, training himself to think clearly under pressure. His visualised scenarios sometimes came true and as he had already rehearsed them in his mind, he was able to deal with them calmly and effectively.[32] We can use this same technique in various challenging and anxiety-inducing contexts; including public speaking, difficult conversations, and physical challenges.

Visualising past successes: When feeling anxious about an upcoming difficult situation, activity, or challenge, it can also be beneficial to put them into context and get a more realistic perspective by recalling previously similar challenges that you may have overcome in the past. As an academic I sometimes had to do live media interviews and often found myself turning down opportunities to discuss my research on radio or television out of fear of making a mistake or embarrassing myself. However, at this point I had done some good live interviews, so in preparation for media appointments I'd remind myself that I'd successfully come through challenges like this in the past, visualising the process. I'd also recall and visualise other challenges I'd overcome in areas of life that weren't related to speaking to the media, but reminded me I had been resilient and resourceful before.

Beyond visualisation: Research has suggested it can be even more beneficial to go beyond just visualising the process before practising in a challenging environment. Individuals and groups that not only visualised a challenge, but also wrote down their objectives, explained to others what they intended to do, and wrote a weekly progress report, were more successful in meeting their objectives than those who didn't.[33] Each added incremental step increased the likelihood of a successful outcome.

Also, as described earlier, visiting a place or venue, if relevant and appropriate, where the challenge or task will take place can be beneficial, and being able to physically practise in that environment can help further. Try to add to the visualisation in as many practical ways as possible. If you are required to wear formal clothes for a talk, visualise and practise it wearing formal clothes. Students taking one of the courses I taught had to do their assessed presentations in formal suits, so I would always allow them to book time in the room that would be used for the assessment, in order for them to at least look around, and practise if they wished. I also encouraged them to dress in the clothes they would be wearing on the day of the presentation, both when practising at home and at the venue. Try to make the visualisations and practice as real as possible.

*

Knowing how we can use different skills and strategies in order to become unstuck or take action is very useful, but in order for us to really grasp them and experience their power, we need to apply them. Then, when we really need to use them, we will have more confidence in our ability to put them into practice and take positive action. So in the next chapter we're going to start taking action and applying the skills we've learned by completing a project.

Chapter 12
The Fear Project

The ultimate aims of this book are to help you overcome anxiety and live with courage. These may seem like huge lofty goals, almost unreachable, but hopefully, as you've been going through the book and trying out the exercises, you've been recognising the thinking and behaviours that make you anxious, and discovering new ones that have a positive influence.

People often think of anxious people as being unambitious, wanting to lead a quiet life, or as not being very motivated, but the truth is most of them are too motivated. Ask them what they want to do and they'll say, *'I should get this entire house cleaned up today.'* or, *'I should start exercising every day.'* *'I need to start making all my own meals from scratch.'* *'I want a job I love.'* *'I'd like to travel and experience new places.'*

Sometimes the goals we automatically select, without thinking, are so great we cannot possibly do them, or at least not in the timeframe we imagine. We get discouraged before we've even really started. This is because massive change feels overwhelming. The challenge of the project in this chapter is to let go of the idea you're going to change your entire life all at once, but understand you can start to take action bit-by-bit, using small incremental steps.

To encourage anxious students to use the skills, strategies, and exercises we've discussed in this book, I often gave them a project to do. The project helped them to practically apply what they had learned, while also making them accountable, but was also designed to be small, manageable, and not too overwhelming.

I wanted to create an evidence-based, step-by-step process, that gave them the courage and motivation to work on and overcome their fears, reconstruct their beliefs, change their mindset, and create an understanding that anxiety and fear need not hold them back. After leaving my post at the university I began developing an online course to help people manage anxiety and fear, and started to work with other organisations and individuals. The student-specific project was then developed to become more inclusive and became known as 'The Fear Project'.

Exercise: The Fear Project

The aim of the fear project is to help you to start moving out of your comfort zone. To tackle some of the small challenges you are facing right now. To begin to take action and get things done, even if these things seem very minor. Beginning with small, manageable behaviours will also allow you to gain momentum, build confidence, create self-belief, and develop a growth mindset: nurturing the belief that you can change your behaviour and the way you respond to anxiety.

It's easy to read through a book like this, maybe try a few exercises, but then put it down and get distracted by responsibilities, chores, tasks, and work; and go no further. Getting started is key.

Step 1 – Consider your fear list
To start the process we're going to create a 'Fear List'. This is a

list of tasks or activities that can be divided into two categories. The first category should include some minor tasks or activities you've been avoiding because you're fearful of doing them – tasks that just need to be done and are never going away – we'll call these 'Avoidance Tasks'.

The second category should comprise of tasks or activities you'd love to be able to do, that create a sense of excitement and inspiration within you, but you've felt unable to do for fearing you may fail, be embarrassed, or haven't had the confidence to try. We'll call these 'Inspirational Tasks'.

Step 2 – Write the list down
Using a table like the one on the next page, take some time to carefully think about what you'd like to include on your list, then write your choices down, and set a date you can realistically complete these tasks by. When I did my first 'Fear List' I included some avoidance tasks that may seem very minor to others, but caused me quite a lot of anxiety (you may see a pattern of the type of activities that made me anxious): calling the dentist to make an appointment, contacting an electrician to fix house lights that had been broken for over a year, booking a service for my car. Similarly, some of the inspirational tasks may not seem very inspirational or anxiety-inducing to many people, but what is most important is how inspirational or anxiety-inducing you find them.

Step 3 – Remembering your best self
At this stage it would be beneficial to look over '*Foundational Exercise 1: Who are you?*' in Chapter 5 of the book. Remember, research suggests when we affirm our most deeply held values — the best parts of our authentic selves – before entering into a potentially challenging or difficult situation, we can reduce our anxiety and be more effective in our behaviour. So going over the core values we wrote about in this exercise will help us to draw strength from who we are before we start to take action.

The Fear List		
Avoidance Tasks	**Date to complete by**	**Completed (✓)**
E.g. Call dentist to arrange appointment		
E.g. Sort out bills that need to be paid		
E.g. Talk to friend about a disagreement		
E.g. Mow lawn		
Inspirational Tasks	**Date to complete by**	**Completed (✓)**
E.g. Enrol in class to learn French		
E.g. Write an article to be published online		
E.g. Start to learn how to paint		

Step 4 –Take action and tackle your fear list

When you start to tackle your Fear List it's likely you're going to have some unhelpful thoughts and uncomfortable feelings. Remember, you need to defuse from unhelpful thoughts, and make room for any uncomfortable feelings that come up, and then engage with the present. The actions of confidence come first and the feelings of confidence come second. Accept, welcome, and then if possible, use your fear (or just allow it to be there).

If you're lacking any skills to do your tasks, just go through the confidence cycle until you're able to complete your task successfully. Go back through the exercises throughout the book to help you. Remember, these are just small tasks, they should be manageable. You won't necessarily require all the skills and techniques we have learned to complete these activities, but the exercise should give you the momentum and motivation to move forward and not to allow anxiety to keep you stuck. Don't be afraid to start very small and unambitiously.

Help! I'm Stuck!: Troubleshooting The Fear Project

What if you feel stuck and unable to complete one, some, or all of the tasks in The Fear Project? What holds us back from doing something we'd really like to do, or from doing uncomfortable things we don't like, but need to do, often making a situation much worse? There are three common reasons, and we've discussed these reasons before.

1. Fusing with our thoughts: the mind hooks us with its thoughts and stories and we get lost in them. These thoughts aren't a problem when we're defused from them, but when we fuse with them they become obstacles.

Antidote: Defusion. Next time you're stuck, ask yourself, 'What am I fusing with? You can notice it, name it and neutralise it, using one of the defusion exercises outlined in Chapter 7, and then engage fully in what you are doing.

2. Excessive goals: if a goal exceeds our resources we will fail. So ask yourself if you're trying to do too much too soon. It's good to dream big, but you also have to be realistic to avoid getting discouraged.

Antidote: Set realistic goals. If a goal exceeds your resources then you have two options:

Firstly, you can pause the original goal and set a new goal to find the necessary resources. If your original goal was to leave your job for a job you love, but you're not qualified to do the job you love, you could set a new goal aimed at earning the necessary qualifications or skills.

Secondly, you could scale down your original goal to a goal that fits the resources you have available. So if you are aiming for a new job, what other job could you do with your current experience, knowledge, and qualifications?

3. Avoiding discomfort: when you step outside of your comfort zone, what happens? You feel discomfort. If you're waiting for your discomfort to go, or not making room for it, you may be waiting a long time. Ask yourself, what thoughts and feelings am I trying to avoid or get rid of?

Antidote: Accept discomfort. Are you willing to make room for the discomfort when you step outside of your comfort zone, and for the difficult emotions and sensations that will arise? Choosing to grow and explore new horizons may bring about many fears, but the alternative is stagnation and personal cost. Accepting the discomfort will also bring a new sense of meaning, purpose, and personal growth.

*

So, getting unstuck will involve defusion, expansion, and engagement, along with overcoming your fear, and if new skills are needed, using the confidence cycle.

Emergency Exercises:
Managing Fight, Flight, or Freeze

Chapter 13
Calming the Anxiety Response

Throughout the course of the book we've talked about what anxiety is, how it develops, when it is useful, and when it becomes a problem. Most of the strategies so far have centred on exercises that change our relationship with anxiety; helping us to manage our anxious thoughts, uncomfortable feelings, and resultant behaviours. We've focused on not allowing anxiety to keep us stuck, hold us back, or stop us from living a meaningful life.

However, what if we're particularly panicked, anxious, angry, or stressed, and really need help right at that very moment? Maybe we feel like we're losing it in a situation in which we feel trapped: sitting at an exam feeling overwhelmed, panicking before a job interview, feeling faint when waiting for a medical appointment, or waking in the middle of the night to a feeling of dread.

This section contains some short and simple exercises that are focused on reducing the physiological symptoms of anxiety. You won't be surprised to learn these exercises are designed to help us switch from the sympathetic nervous system, which we should all know by now, is very aggressive, to the parasympathetic nervous system, which is much calmer.

We described the role the amygdala plays in anxiety in Chapter 3. We said it is involved in both pathways, and is the part of the brain that initiates the emergency arousal system: the fight, flight, or freeze response. Once the challenge or emergency response has kicked in, whether it is through the thought-based cortex pathway telling the amygdala to react, or directly through the reactive pathway of the amygdala itself, our ability to think and respond to the anxiety reaction in a logical way is very limited. So recognising the arousal response and understanding what is about to happen before it occurs, or just after it starts, is vital to responding to it appropriately and reducing anxiety quickly.

Once the emergency response is up and running, the chances of strategically thinking our way out of it are very limited. Indeed our cortex can misinterpret why these symptoms are occurring and convince us something dangerous is happening or going to happen. This can heighten our anxiety response further and we can become trapped in a negative feedback loop.

Remember, when our emergency arousal system is activated, the sympathetic nervous system is energised and stress hormones such as cortisol and adrenaline are released. This produces a rapid number of physiological responses that include: increased heart rate, elevated blood pressure, rapid breathing, blood flowing to the extremities, slowed digestion, and increased sweating. This response is extremely useful to us when we're in danger, providing us with extra strength and alertness, giving us a better chance to escape more swiftly, fight more powerfully, or freeze and hide away more effectively.

All of this happens within a fraction of a second, before we consciously know what is happening. It's wired this way to help save our lives, and so can't be based on any higher thinking; there is no time to ponder strategies of how and best to react. It's a vital, life saving, hardwired system that we need when we're in genuine danger, but it's not so helpful when we react in this way when giving a presentation in front of an audience, noticing our neighbour's car is parked on our grass, or opening a letter from our bank telling us our account is overdrawn.

So when we are experiencing the physiological symptoms of anxiety, triggered by the fight, flight or freeze response, we need to be aware of this, and target the amygdala directly. We're going to look at two different categories of the physiological anxiety response and suggest exercises that can help both; firstly the aggressive **fight or flight response**; and then the **freeze response** to anxiety.

Fight or Flight Exercises

The following exercises are intentionally short and simple. Remember, they are designed to help you switch quickly from a defensive and aggressive state, to a much calmer one. These exercises should be practised if you're feeling particularly panicked, anxious, angry, or stressed, and you don't want to behave or feel that way. As with all of the other exercises included in the book, the more you practise them, the quicker they will work and the more effective they will be. Just read through the exercises, try each one out, and then pick one or two that work best for you and use them when needed.

Fight or Flight Exercise 1: Three Deep Breaths

This exercise is quick and effective. By slowing down breathing and taking deep breaths we can direct our body to switch from the sympathetic system's stress response to the parasympathetic system's relax response.

Step 1
Take a short, strong, but gentle, inward breath through your nose for two seconds and then breath out slowly through your mouth for 5-7 seconds.

Step 2

Repeat step 1 another two or three times. The response is almost immediate and surprisingly powerful. If you find you're still experiencing powerful physical anxiety symptoms, try to breathe normally for about a minute and then repeat the exercise again.

*

Fight or Flight Exercise 2: Getting Present

This exercise is designed to bring you into the present moment and out of thoughts and feelings of panic:

Step 1

Sounds: For one minute notice what sounds you can hear in the environment around you. Rather than striving to hear sounds, allow the sounds to come to you. Each time your attention wanders away from the sounds and back to your thinking, gently and with compassion, bring your attention back to the sounds.

Step 2

Objects: For one minute notice up to three objects you can see in your environment in as great a detail as possible (shape, colour, texture etc.). Imagine you are a visitor from another planet and have never seen these objects before. Each time your attention wanders away from the objects and back to your thinking, gently and with compassion, bring your attention back to the object.

Step 3

Now try to engage in the present moment and focus on what is happening in your immediate environment.

*

Fight or Flight Exercise 3: The Pause

This exercise is useful when we feel like we are losing control of our emotions, particularly when we're getting lost in our reaction to a person, situation, or event. This exercise calms the amygdala and gives us greater access to our prefrontal cortex, enabling us to act more calmly and effectively.

An audio version of this exercise can be found here: https://soundcloud.com/dr-matt-lewis/the-pause-mp3

The Angry Sergeant
Before outlining the steps, I'll summarise a true story told by Tara Brach, a psychologist and meditation teacher, that illustrates the power and effectiveness of the exercise.[34]

She describes how a Sergeant in United States Army called into a supermarket on his way home from a mindfulness-based anger management course. He was in a rush to get home and got very irritated as he stood waiting in a queue to pay for his groceries. There was a woman in front of him who was holding a baby, waiting to pay for only a few items. The Sergeant thought the woman should have gone to one of the express checkouts and not clogged up the queue he was in. To make matters worse, when the woman was being served, she handed the baby to the cashier and they stood chatting for a while. He felt his irritation and anger growing, but then remembered one of the exercises from his anger management course.

He paused and then asked himself what was going on inside his head at that moment; he tried to be aware of the story that was playing in his mind, and observe what he was thinking and feeling. He noticed anger, and underneath the anger he noticed anxiety about being late, and underneath the anxiety he became aware of a fear of losing control. He stayed with this anger and discomfort for a while and found a little space. In that small gap he had created he noticed how lovely the baby was and how much the two women were enjoying her.

When he got to the front of the queue he remarked to the cashier that the baby was adorable. "Oh thank you." the cashier said, "Actually that's my little girl. My husband was killed in Afghanistan last year so my mother brings her by a few times a day so we have a little time together."

This illustrates if we sometimes don't pause and deepen our attention, we can find ourselves constantly caught up in the stories in our head, living out patterns that separate us from our best selves and from others, and often make difficult situations worse.

Step 1
Pause. Stop for a moment. Breathe. Notice your breathing for 10 to 20 seconds.

Step 2
Notice what is going on inside your mind and body. What stories are you telling yourself? What emotions are there? What is happening in your body? Observe your thoughts and emotions and look for some space. Are you tense? Notice how your body feels.

Step 3
Now bring your attention to the present moment. What is happening around you in your environment. What can you see and hear? Try to engage with what is happening around you without judging.

*

Fight or Flight Exercise 4: The Bell Hand

This exercise involves focusing intently on your dominant hand while opening and closing it. It's an effective exercise for focusing your attention away from unhelpful thoughts and on to the present moment, activating the calming parasympathetic nervous system.

The movement involves softening the palm of the hand by drawing the fingers inward toward the palm, but neither closing the hand into a fist, nor totally stretching out the palm and fingers. Instead the focus is on the gentle opening and closing movement of the fingers and softening of the palm, which can be coordinated with breathing.

Step 1
So start with the palm of your dominant hand open and flat. Exhale and slowly and gently draw your fingers and thumb inward, whilst keeping them straight (so you're not making a fist), until your fingers and thumb meet. See the photo below. Focus your attention intently on the movement and how it feels.

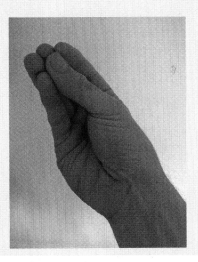

Step 2

Then as you inhale, slowly open your hand again. Repeat this until you start to feel calm. If you attention wanders away, just gently bring it back to focusing on the movements of your hand.

*

Fight or Flight Exercise 5:
Focus on the Soles of Your Feet

You can do this exercise standing or sitting down. If sitting on a chair, adjust your spine so it is straight but not rigid. Your eyes can be open or shut (eyes shut is normally best but if you're unable to do this as you're not in private, keep your eyes open and lower your gaze).

Focus on the Feet

Focus your attention on the sensation of your feet on the ground. Notice the exact sensations, the weight, temperature, tingling, the feeling of your shoes, or nothing at all if that is the case. Notice when your mind takes over with its commentary and as soon as it does, note where it took you, and then bring your focus back to your feet. Keep bringing your attention back to your feet until about two minutes has gone by.

*

Fight or Flight Exercise 6: R.A.I.N

We can use the acronym R.A.I.N. to help us find some space when dealing with difficult emotions.

Step 1

Recognition – When feeling overwhelmed it's difficult to think clearly, it feels as if your head is full of red mist. Firstly, just recognise whatever you can within the swirling mist; such as anxiety, fear, rage or sadness. Just merely identifying an emotion means you're regulating it; you're using your prefrontal cortex to calm the aroused limbic system.

Step 2
Acceptance – All emotions are okay, the harm is done in the way you think about them. Whatever the feeling is, it is just a feeling, you don't have to act on it. Let it pass through, because in the next second it changes anyway. Let go of the shame and blame, it will never get you anywhere other than back to being locked into unhelpful thinking.

Step 3
Investigation – Focus your attention into wherever the emotional pain is in your body. As soon as you tune into the sensation in the body, the story inside your head changes. Investigate inside: is your chest tight? Your stomach churning? Your jaw clenched? If you register nothing, that's fine too.

Step 4
Non-Identification – Step away from the emotions and give them space knowing this will pass too. Stop the struggling. With this distancing, you're developing self-regulation, reducing the intensity. You're focusing on the raw sensations rather than the thoughts behind them and the 'whys' and 'wherefores'. You won't immediately snap out of your anger, anxiety, or stress, but you will give yourself a small gap, enabling you to reflect in the midst of it all. The more you practise, the faster you get at identifying and exploring your emotions.

*

The Freeze Response

When discussing the fight, flight, or freeze response, the 'freeze' part of the arousal system is often overlooked. If the brain assesses, accurately or not, fighting or fleeing the situation is not an option, or the traumatic threat is ongoing, the limbic system can simultaneously activate the parasympathetic nervous system (the calmer state), causing a state of freezing called 'tonic immobility' – like a deer caught in the headlights, or a rabbit playing dead when spotted by a hunting dog. This can happen in situations in which you don't have enough hormone-assisted strength or speed to respond to an overwhelming emergency by fighting or running away.

When this happens we can sometimes dissociate from being in the present moment; this can help us not to feel the overwhelming enormity of what is happening; and hormones, including endorphins, can be released, acting as an analgesic, reducing the pain of mental or physical injuries. Additionally, if you're not putting up a fight or running away, the person or animal attacking you might lose interest in continuing their attack, or if you can't make the attacker stop by fighting or fleeing, the brain thinks it is a better option to disappear within itself and block out what is too overwhelming and frightening to take in.

Just as with the fight or flight response, the freeze response can also be triggered in relatively safe situations. Some people seem more prone to the freeze response and are more likely to be withdrawn and avoidant rather than experience feelings of panic. However, research has indicated if we use an active coping strategy when we feel frozen, withdrawn, and immobilised like this, we can undo the freeze response and train our brains to respond in this way in similar situations in the future.[35]

*

Freeze Response Exercise:
Do Something Active

Do Something Active

This exercise may seem very simple, but it can be difficult to start in the middle of a freeze response. Research suggests you should find something active you can do during the moment you feel frozen, almost anything active: do a jigsaw puzzle, tidy up, or call someone on the phone. Social activities can be particularly helpful when feeling frozen, indeed anything that involves pleasurable interactions with others. The key is to do something that interrupts the freeze response of the amygdala.

Often when experiencing the freeze response, people feel too anxious to do anything, they may often stay in bed, avoiding work or other commitments, but by shifting the amygdala to a more active response, they find the interruption creates some momentum and allows them to engage in activities that may have seemed overwhelming beforehand.

Plan Ahead

It can be difficult to think of something active to do while in the middle of a freeze response, so plan ahead. When you are functioning well and feel in control, think of activities you could easily do, are readily available, and make a list. Then, when you do feel immobile, it will be easier to choose something active without having to think too much about it. Try to raise your awareness of experiencing the freeze response, notice when it is happening and then take action.

Chapter 14
Panic Attacks

Panic attacks can last from anywhere between thirty seconds to thirty minutes and can be so distressing sufferers sometimes have the feeling they are losing control or about to die. The experience can be one of extreme agitation, terror, fury, or immobilisation, accompanied by extreme symptoms of the fight, flight, or freeze response; racing heart, rapid breathing, trembling, shaking, nausea, numbness, tight chest, difficulty swallowing, and hot flushes or chills. Episodes can return in waves, are frightening and often exhausting.

Panic attacks are normally initiated when the amygdala responds to a trigger in the environment that the person may or may not even be aware of. They can be triggered by situations, smells, sounds, or feelings; based on deeply held fears or associational memory. They can often occur at inappropriate times and are due to an overreaction by the amygdala, often in response to a cue or trigger that doesn't pose any real threat or danger. If there was a real danger or emergency then the physiological responses would be appropriate and helpful.

Most people will experience some sort of panic attack once or twice in their lives, but those who have more regular panic attacks can start to fear them, and this anxiety can become a self-fulfilling prophecy, with an attack being triggered simply by the fear of having one. For example, a person may once have had a panic attack at the cinema, so during their next visit to the cinema they fear the same thing happening again, which can start to trigger panic attack symptoms. This can lead to the person avoiding the cinema altogether, and then avoiding other public places in the future. This is the type of *Escape Avoidance Learning* we discussed in Chapter 4, and it can lead to agoraphobia and other clinical anxiety disorders.

Important: Don't Try to Escape the Situation!

When suffering from a panic attack it's vital you resist the strong impulse to escape the situation. Although panic attacks are very frightening and uncomfortable they can't physically hurt you. Fleeing from the situation may make you feel better in the short-term but in the long-term it will reinforce the power of the attacks, and make it more difficult to overcome them.

We discussed earlier in the book that the amygdala learns from experience. So staying in the situation will help the amygdala to learn that the situation is safe and it doesn't need to react in the same way in the future. While this is much easier said than done, it would be beneficial to see these situations as opportunities to work on changing the anxiety response; reducing and eventually eliminating further episodes.

Although it is very difficult to calm a panic attack through cortex-based logical thinking, there are some things you can do during an attack that will help reduce the ability of the cortex to create the conditions in which the panic attack can get worse:

1. Understand it's only a feeling: Interpreting the symptoms of a panic attack as life threatening can cause the symptoms to get a lot worse. So it's important to try to recognise you are having a panic attack and nothing more. This will ensure you don't add fuel to the flames.

2. Don't worry about what other people think: In the middle of a panic attack people often feel embarrassed and worried other people are judging them. Don't let your cortex try to predict what other people are thinking, it is probably wrong anyway, and it will only add to the stress and panic.

3. Don't focus on the panic attack: Try not to obsess about when a panic attack may come. Not worrying about panic attacks is one of the best ways to avoid them. Constantly focusing on bodily sensations like sweating and butterflies in the stomach, can lead you to thinking yourself into a panic. While again, this is easier said than done, if you do find yourself thinking or worrying about a possible panic attack, use one of the defusion exercises in Chapter 7 and then focus your attention on the present moment. With practice these defusion techniques will get easier and work faster.

*

So what should we do if we start to recognise symptoms of a panic attack starting, or if we suddenly become aware we're caught up in one? How can we best cope? While we can't immediately stop the attack, there are a number of strategies that can reduce the power of the symptoms and also shorten the duration of the attack. These strategies are, of course, designed to help us switch from the aggressive sympathetic nervous system to the calmer parasympathetic nervous system.

Always keep in mind that in order to eliminate or greatly reduce future panic attacks you need to try to avoid escaping the situation. This can be difficult at first and will require patience and courage, but with time and practice it will get easier. Experiencing short-term fear will provide you with long-term peace.

Panic Attack Exercise 1:
Deep Abdominal Breathing

An audio version of this exercise can be found here:

https://soundcloud.com/dr-matt-lewis/calming-panic-attacks-audio-exercise

Deep breathing can be effective when having a panic attack as many of the symptoms we experience are related to hyperventilation, which is fast and shallow breathing. When we go into hyperventilation, we breathe out carbon dioxide too quickly, resulting in low levels of it in the body. This is identified immediately by the amygdala and triggers a highly reactive response. This is why people who are having a panic attack are advised to breathe into a paper bag; the bag will capture the expelled carbon dioxide, allowing it to be inhaled back into the bloodstream.

By using conscious deep breathing we can relax the amygdala and prevent hyperventilation, or bring it under control after it has been triggered.

Step 1
Sit as comfortable as you possibly can, placing one hand on the chest and one hand on the stomach. If you're unable to sit down you can still do this exercise standing up.

Take a deep breath in and see which part of your body rises. People often find that their chest rises as they breathe in. However, effective abdominal breathing will cause your stomach to expand as you inhale and retract as you exhale. Your chest shouldn't move much at all.

Step 2
Try to focus on breathing deeply in a way that expands your

stomach as you fill your lungs with air. You should feel your stomach rising underneath your hand when you breathe in. Many people tend to pull their stomachs in as they inhale, which keeps the diaphragm from expanding downward effectively. So focus your attention on your stomach rising as you inhale.

Important Note

Some people find focusing on breathing increases their anxiety, especially if they have asthma or other conditions that cause breathing difficulties. If you find the breathing exercises uncomfortable use the other recommended exercises instead.

*

Panic Attack Exercise 2:
Progressive Muscle Relaxation

A panic attack often results in muscle tension throughout the body, and tight muscles also tend to increase amygdala activation. So learning and practicing muscle relaxation techniques will help to shorten panic attacks and make them less likely. If you are prone to panic attacks, you should practise the following exercise regularly so you are able to use it quickly and effectively when experiencing severe anxiety.

The exercise uses a two-step process. Firstly, you systematically tense particular muscle groups in your body, and then you release the tension and notice how your muscles feel when you relax them. Anxious people are often so tense throughout the day they may not recognise what being physically relaxed feels like. Through practice you can learn to distinguish between the feelings of a tensed muscle and a completely relaxed muscle.

Then you can begin to quickly initiate this relaxed state at the first sign of the muscle tension that accompanies your feelings of anxiety. By tensing and releasing, you learn not only what relaxation feels like, but also to recognise when you are starting to get tense

When first trying the exercise it should take around 10-15 minutes to complete. Or you can just practise with different muscle groups for 2-3 minutes at a time. You don't have to be feeling anxious when you practise it, practising it when you are calm can make it easier to do when feeling anxious or starting to panic.

Step 1: Getting ready
If possible, find a quiet, comfortable place to sit, then close your eyes and let your body go loose. You can lie down, but this will increase your chances of falling asleep. Although relaxing before bed can improve your sleep, the goal of this exercise is to learn to relax while awake. Take between three and five slow, deep breaths before you begin.

Step 2: Apply muscle tension to a specific part of the body
Focus on a specific muscle group, such as your left hand. Take a slow, deep breath and squeeze the muscles as hard as you can for about 5 seconds. It is important to really feel the tension in the muscles, which may even cause a bit of discomfort or shaking. In this instance, you would be making a tight fist with your left hand. It is easy to accidentally tense other surrounding muscles (for example, the shoulder or arm), so try to only tense the muscles you are targeting. Isolating muscle groups gets easier with practice.

Step 3: Relaxing the tense muscles
After about 5 seconds, let all the tightness leave the tensed muscles. Breathe out as you do this step. You should feel the muscles become loose and limp as the tension flows out. Deliberately focus on, and notice the difference between, the tension and relaxation. This is the most important part of the whole exercise. Remain in this relaxed state for about 10

seconds, and then move on to the next muscle group.

Step 4: Repeat the tension-relaxation steps with the other groups
To make it easier to remember, you can start with your feet and systematically move up (or if you prefer, you can do it in the reverse order, from your forehead down to your feet).
For example:
Foot (curl your toes downward)
Lower leg and foot (tighten your calf muscle by pulling toes towards you)
Entire leg (squeeze thigh muscles while doing above)
(Repeat on other side of body)

Hand (clench your fist)
Entire right arm (tighten your biceps by drawing your forearm up towards your shoulder and 'make a muscle', while clenching fist)
(Repeat on other side of body)

Buttocks (tighten by pulling your buttocks together)
Abdomen (suck your stomach in)
Chest (tighten by taking a deep breath)
Neck and shoulders (raise your shoulders up to touch your ears)
Mouth (open your mouth wide enough to stretch the hinges of your jaw)
Eyes (clench your eyelids tightly shut)
Forehead (raise your eyebrows as far as you can)

Step 5: Relax
After completing all of the muscle groups, take one minute to enjoy the state of relaxation.

It can take time to learn to relax the body and notice the difference between tension and relaxation. At first it can feel uncomfortable to be focusing on your body, but this can become quite enjoyable over time.

Panic Attack Exercise 3:
Quick Tense and Relax

Once you have become familiar with Exercise 2, you can begin to practise a very short version of progressive muscle relaxation. In this approach, you learn how to tense larger groups of muscles, which takes even less time. These muscle groups are:

1. Lower limbs (feet and legs)
2. Stomach and chest
3. Arms, shoulders, and neck
4. Face

So instead of working with just one specific muscle group at a time (e.g., your stomach), you can focus on the complete group (your stomach and chest). You can start by focusing on your breathing during the tension and relaxation.

When doing this shortened version, it can be helpful to say a certain word or phrase to yourself as you slowly exhale (such as "relax", "let go", "stay calm", "peace" etc.). This word or phrase will become associated with a relaxed state; eventually, saying this word alone can bring on a calm feeling. This can be beneficial during times when it would be hard to take the time to go through all the steps of progressive muscle relaxation.

*

Panic Attack Exercise 4: Release Only

You can further shorten the time you take to relax your muscles by becoming familiar with the 'release only' technique. One of the benefits of tensing and releasing muscles is that you learn to recognise what tense and relaxed muscles feel like.

Once comfortable with this you can start doing 'release only', which involves removing the 'tension' step of the exercise. For example, instead of tensing your stomach and chest before relaxing them, try just relaxing the muscles. At first, the feeling of relaxation might feel less intense than when you tensed the muscles beforehand, but with practice, the release-only technique can be just as relaxing.

Remember it's vital to practise progressive muscle relaxation often, feeling anxious or not. This will make the exercise more effective when you really need to use it. It may seem a little tedious at first, but it can become a very effective tool for treating anxiety and reducing the power and duration of panic attacks.

*

Panic Attack Exercise 5: Physical Exercise

If you're in a place where you're able to move about when having a panic attack it would be very beneficial to pace or exercise. Remember, this is the emergency arousal system kicking in, preparing your body to fight or flee, so physical exertion is exactly what your body is ready to do. If your sympathetic nervous system is activated, you can put it to use as nature intended. If you run or walk briskly when you feel anxious, you'll make use of the muscles that have been prepared for action. Exercising will also burn off excess adrenaline and make use of the glucose released into the bloodstream by the stress response.

Many of the physical sensations you experience when exercising are similar to the way the body reacts when the emergency arousal system has been activated; increased heart rate and blood pressure, faster breathing. So exercising can also be a form of exposure therapy, allowing you to experience and get used to these types of physical changes, making us less afraid and more accepting of the sensations over time.

Moving Forward

Chapter 15
What Next?

I hope this book has given you an insight into your anxiety, and provided you with the tools to help you find peace, act with courage, and live a life closely aligned to your values. As you became immersed in the detail of each chapter you may have found yourself losing sight of the overall structure and strategy of the book, so we'll summarise the structure again over the next few pages. Firstly, let's review the key messages relayed in the first five parts of the book:

• Evaluate your beliefs and nurture the mindset that it is possible to change and grow.

• Raise awareness of how and why your anxiety develops in order to manage it effectively.

• Understand your values, be your best self, and live authentically.

• Train your mind to effectively manage your thoughts and emotions.

• Accept discomfort and courageously take action to create the life you want.

Now let's summarise what we've learned in the previous chapters in a little more detail and then discuss how we can bring it all together, take the next steps, and outline some 'powerful essentials' that can help propel us forward.

MINDSET

One of the main aims of the book was to help nurture a growth mindset; to create a set of beliefs that acknowledges change is possible. Remember changing the way you think about anxiety is the first step to overcoming it; not all anxiety and stress is bad, it can be helpful in many situations. However, when anxiety is detrimental; through learning, effort, and application; we can change, grow, and transform our relationship with it. Anxiety is inevitable but it shouldn't stop us from living with courage and being our best selves.

SURVIVAL SYSTEMS

Our survival systems were developed to keep us safe from danger and motivated to survive, but the way these systems interact can sometimes cause us to feel anxious, stressed and unhappy. Our *negativity bias* developed in harsh conditions but still operates in a similar way in today's relatively safe environments, meaning we sometimes react to relatively safe or neutral situations as if they are life or death.

The negativity bias also interacts with our *emergency arousal system* – the fight, flight or freeze response – which can be triggered by the negative thoughts we have. This stress response didn't evolve to be continually activated, but only when needed for survival, or to help us in challenging situations. This continuous activation can set us up for many physical and mental anxiety-related ailments.

We also evolved to *pursue pleasure and avoid pain*, and as a result we can get hooked on constantly seeking these things, and when we don't have the perfect conditions that allow us to experience them, or fear we could lose them, it makes us feel distressed. So we're not only impacted by immediate threats to our survival, but also the fear we won't get what we evolved to seek out.

On top of these hardwired survival systems, we have also discovered learning changes the brain through *neuroplasticity*. So the neural pathways involved in our anxious thinking can become stronger, like a riverbed that deepens over time.

With the interaction of these survival systems and the reinforcing of anxious thinking by neuroplasticity, it's not difficult to understand why life can be very challenging and often make us feel anxious. However, there are exercises and practices that can make us aware of these unhelpful thinking patterns and retrain the brain not to automatically respond in this way.

PATHWAYS TO ANXIETY

Anxiety can originate from two different areas of the brain: anxiety produced as a result of our thoughts is initiated in the cortex, and anxiety produced by our reaction to what is happening in our environment is initiated in the amygdala. We referred to these two pathways as the *thought pathway* and the *reactive pathway*.

We can learn to manage our thought pathway anxiety through practising the mindfulness skills of *defusion*, *expansion* and *engagement*. Reactive pathway anxiety can be managed by raising our awareness of it – understanding our reactions are result of our amygdala being triggered by our environment. We can also eliminate or reduce reactive pathway anxiety further by learning through experience.

ANXIETY DISORDERS

Everyone experiences anxiety from time to time. It can often be situation specific or last for a short period of time. However, sometimes anxiety can feel more permanent, impacting nearly every part of our lives.

Anxiety disorders often develop through *Escape Avoidance Learning*. This occurs when we try to escape the unpleasant feelings by leaving the situation causing the anxiety. Doing this does relieve our anxiety, but also makes us more likely to repeat this behaviour in the future by escaping any situation that causes us anxiety. This is called *negative reinforcement*, and the avoidance behaviour it encourages can extend to other situations and environments and affect more and more of our everyday lives.

However, we can learn to increase our capacity to bear anxiety and be more accepting of the uncomfortable feelings it brings. By doing this we can change our relationship with anxiety, transform our behaviour, and break the vicious cycle.

CREATING A FOUNDATION

By taking a step back and assessing who we really are, how we live our lives, and how we could change them for the better; we can build a foundation that will help us to stand strong when faced with the challenge of changing our relationship with anxiety. When we affirm our most deeply held values, we can reduce our anxiety, becoming less defensive and more open and authentic in our behaviour.

We also need to ensure we manage our energy and take time to do the activities and practices that nourish us. Without the things that nourish us, stress increases and we give up more and more of the activities that replenish us. As a result we're only left with stressors that deplete our resources and we can become exhausted or burnt out. It's easy to get sucked into this process because we often have pressing demands, and when we do, the more pleasurable things in life tend to seem optional and are easier to give up.

Although it may feel counterintuitive at the time, in order to do the pressing things well and to maintain our wellbeing, we need to make space for replenishment and nourishment. This will give us the extra time, energy and perspective needed for the challenging parts of our lives.

CALMING THE MIND

Exercises and practices that calm the mind are beneficial for managing anxiety initiated in both in the cortex (thought pathway anxiety) and in the amygdala (reactive pathway anxiety). Research on mindfulness practices has also testified to various positive changes in both brain functioning and structure. When done consistently, mindfulness practices can alter the brain in a way that: improves our focus and attention, slows down age-related mental decline, and helps us to manage our emotions.

Meditation is one of the most popular mindfulness practices. It is not a religion and doesn't have to be performed as a spiritual practice; it is evidence-based mental training. It can be a relatively short practice and done when sitting, standing, walking, or doing a routine task. You don't have to have a certain type of mind to meditate; it is not about emptying your head of thoughts, but rather about learning to focus your attention on one thing and consistently bringing your attention back to the thing when the mind wanders.

The benefits of meditation to your mental health may be apparent very early on and will grow with time. Guided meditations can help you when you first begin, and can also be helpful when you are more experienced, but you should also soon be able to meditate without a guided meditation recording or an app.

DEALING WITH ANXIOUS THOUGHTS AND FEELINGS

Acceptance and Commitment Therapy (ACT) teaches a radical way of responding to unhelpful thoughts and feelings that may seem counterintuitive. The ACT approach suggests we can reduce the influence of unhelpful thoughts and anxious feelings without trying to get rid of them; this method works even though it makes no effort whatsoever to reduce, challenge, eliminate, or change negative thoughts.

Negative thoughts are only considered problematic if we get caught up in them, give them all of our attention, treat them as the absolute truth, allow them to control us, or get in a fight with them. The ACT approach teaches three key skills to help us effectively manage thoughts and feelings that cause anxiety: *defusion, expansion, and engagement.*

- When we *defuse* or separate from thoughts, we become aware they are nothing more or less than words and pictures, and can have little or no effect on us, even if they are true.

- When practising *expansion*, we open up and make room for emotions, sensations and feelings. We accept they are there, and allow them to pass through without having an impact on our behaviour. The more space we can give the difficult feelings, the smaller their influence and impact on our lives.

- *Engagement* is being present and actively involved in what we are doing – not lost in our thoughts. Being anxious is not a problem but disengaging from our experience is.

TAKING ACTION

We often think before we are able to do anything properly we have to get rid of the fear of doing it; we simply can't function well when we are experiencing fear. However, there is no way of expanding our comfort zone without stepping outside it and feeling fear. Fear is not a sign of weakness, it's a sign we are pushing our boundaries and progressing.

More often than not, fear won't debilitate us, but focusing on the fear will. Fear doesn't hold us back, but our attitude to fear does. When we're in a real-life challenging situation that doesn't require us to fight, flee, or freeze, there are a number of strategies we can use when fear rises up.

- Firstly we need to *accept it*. We can't numb, push away, or eliminate fear when it arises. Battling or arguing with fear will only take our attention away from the situation or task in hand.

- We should also *welcome it*. Fear evolved to help keep us safe in challenging situations, to alert us to risks, and to prime us for action. It means well and is on our side.

- Finally, we can *use it*. When we feel fear and our sympathetic nervous system initiates the fight, flight, or fear response, our senses get heightened, our reflexes quicken, we get greater strength, and our body is energised and ready for action.

THE CONFIDENCE CYCLE

There are no magic bullets or mystical shortcuts to feeling anxiety-free and supremely confident when learning a skill or entering a new situation. However, we can feel confident about doing almost anything. We've used the confidence cycle many times before, when learning all of life's basic skills and also many of the skills we now take for granted: from walking and talking, to learning to drive, to operating a computer.

The Confidence Cycle involves repeating the following four steps until we become good at whatever we have set our sights on. We need to 1. practise the skills required, 2. apply them effectively in a real life challenging environment, 3. assess the results, and 4. modify the skills as needed. Then we start again at the first step until we reach the standard of skill needed. Visualisation can also be a powerful additional tool to use alongside the confidence cycle.

THE FEAR PROJECT

The Fear Project is an evidence-based, step-by-step process, to help you to start moving out of your comfort zone; to tackle some of the small challenges you are facing; to begin to take action and get things done, even if these things seem very minor. Small, manageable behaviours allow us to gain momentum, build confidence, create self-belief, and develop a growth mindset. The project involves creating a 'fear list' of avoidance and inspirational tasks, and then using the skills learned throughout the book to take action and tackle each task.

CALMING ANXIETY RESPONSES AND PANIC ATTACKS

The final chapters focused on how we can cope with the more extreme mental and physiological responses to anxiety. What we should do when we're particularly panicked, anxious, angry, or stressed, and need help immediately.

We included a number of short and simple exercises, focused on reducing the physiological symptoms of anxiety, designed to help us switch from the aggressive sympathetic nervous system to the calmer parasympathetic nervous system. The exercises are tailored to either the fight and flight response to anxiety, or the freeze response to anxiety. Controlling our breathing and becoming aware of what is happening in the present moment, are particularly effective for controlling physical symptoms and unhelpful thoughts.

Panic attacks are the most severe response to anxiety. When experiencing a panic attack it's important we don't try to escape the situation as this will reinforce the power of the attacks, and make it more difficult to overcome them in the future. We can manage panic attacks by being aware they are not life threatening, not worrying about what other people think, and not focusing on the panic attack. We can also help reduce and eventually eliminate the symptoms of an attack by practising abdominal breathing, learning muscle relaxation, and engaging in physical exercise.

*

The Road Ahead

The challenge now is for you to weave the practices and exercises into your everyday life in a way that is sustainable in the long-term. In order to do this you will need to try out the different exercises and decide which ones work best for you. Choose the exercises you find most effective, enjoyable, and will fit best into your daily routine. Keep in my mind you do not have to stick rigidly to your original choices; you may find as time goes by your choices and preferences change. Different experiences and different demands on your life may make some exercises more applicable at different times. So be open, aware, and flexible.

I would suggest you check-in on your values and reaffirm them often (*Foundational Exercise 1: Who Are You?*). We need reminding of who we are and what we stand for on a regular basis, particularly when we're facing challenges or going through a stressful period of life. Similarly, be aware of your energy levels, particularly when life is busy, and take time to consider if you're living a balanced life that includes activities and experiences that nourish you.

Continue to practise the mindfulness exercises, these will strengthen your ability to calm your mind. The benefits of the exercises will build over time, so I would suggest you practise them daily, or at least on a regular basis. Consider extending your meditation sessions to up to 20 minutes. After some practice you may feel you can meditate without audio guidance, but use the guidance for as long as you find it helpful. I still use guided meditation in my everyday practice.

When anxiety arises, remember to use the mindfulness skills you've learned – defusion, expansion and engagement – to effectively deal with unhelpful thoughts and uncomfortable feelings – it gets much easier and more intuitive as time goes by. Don't allow your anxiety to stop you from growing; keep seeking out challenges that enrich your life and don't let anxious feelings keep you from tackling the difficulties life throws at us.

The Fear Project will have encouraged you to start small and gain momentum. Use this strategy to overcome the paralysis that small and uncomfortable problems can cause, but don't be afraid to dream big and set larger goals. Be ambitious, break the goals down into small steps, tame your fear, accept the discomfort, and use the confidence cycle to learn new skills and overcome obstacles.

One Last Exercise

This book is primarily concerned with overcoming anxiety and being able to function in life again. It is about finding out who you are and taking small steps to become unstuck and move forward. It was written with the intention of not being overwhelming for the reader.

However, in this one last task, I want you to use some of the exercises we've done, and skills we've learned, to think bigger, and to consider where you want to be heading over the next year or so. Most of us are so busy surviving we never consider where our lives are going. When this is the case other people or circumstances design our lives for us.

Exercise: Poster – My Next Year

Set one hour aside to do this exercise, although it may take you much less time to complete. You can also do the exercise over a few days or longer if you find that easier. – just keep going back to the poster until you feel it's complete.

Step 1
Take an A4 size sheet of paper, and across the top, write your name, today's date, and the date in one year's time. E.g. *"Matt Lewis – 1st June 2017 to 1st June 2018"*

Step 2

At the top of the poster write a mission statement for the next year of your life. In other words, what is your purpose over the next year? What do you want to achieve over the next 12 months? Where are you heading? What do you want the next year to look like? The statement should be a brief paragraph containing four to five sentences. It can be about anything from developing your career, to nurturing your relationships, to learning to paint, to spending more time outdoors.

Step 3

Now reduce your mission statement to one sentence and write it down in the middle of your poster, underneath the full mission statement from Step 2. The sentence should really capture the essence of your mission statement. It may take a little while to do, but distilling it down into one sentence will help to clarify your thinking. You can keep this mission statement sentence private (or you can share it if you wish), but write it in such a way you are able to remember it and could easily communicate it to others. It's designed to be an easily identifiable trigger for your focus over the coming year.

Step 4

At the bottom of the poster write down your top 4 primary goals for the next year. This is your action plan for achieving your mission statement, so it should be very practical. Ensure each goal is:

- Specific – target a specific task, rather than being general or ambiguous.
- Measurable – clear enough so you know when it has been achieved.
- Attainable – can be realistically achieved given the available resources.
- Relevant – it fits in with, and is connected to, your mission statement.
- Time Bound – it can be achieved within one year.

Put the poster in a place when you see it regularly, to remind you of where your focus should be. If, as time goes by, you feel you have clarified your mission statement or goals further, or even changed them due to further understanding or a change of circumstances, don't be afraid to make alterations to it. Use the mindfulness skills to help you make progress, tame your fear when needed, and use the confidence cycle to learn new skills.

Chapter 16
Powerful Essentials

I wanted to keep this book short, simple and manageable, with the intention of not overwhelming people with a whole host of changes that need to be implemented over a short period of time; this is a recipe for failure. However, it would be remiss of me not to mention a few of the most freely available, cost-effective, and important contributors to overall wellbeing and positive mental health: sleep, physical exercise, media diet, and social interaction. These powerful essentials are often discounted or ignored as people look for a shortcut to good mental health or a magic bullet for peak performance.

Sleep

Getting enough sleep is crucial to both our physical and mental health. We can implement every other mental and physical health strategy to perfection, but if we're not getting enough sleep we will never be at our best. Research indicates that sufficient sleep has a large positive effect on a whole host of physical and mental aspects of our health, including: emotion regulation, cognitive thinking, decision making, attention, memory, and it also plays a large role in protecting the immune system.[36]

Until recently we have known very little about what happens in the brain when we sleep, and although we still have much to learn, we are starting to understand more about what happens when we go to bed at night.

THE SLEEP CYCLE

We now know we cycle through different periods of sleep several times a night, and in the final stage of each of these cycles we enter Rapid Eye Movement sleep (REM), the period when dreaming occurs. It's thought REM sleep is particularly important for our wellbeing, as it's involved in replenishing our neurotransmitters, cleaning out toxins, and consolidating our memories. Research has also indicated those who have more REM sleep tend to have lower amygdala reactivity, and as a result, less anxiety.[37] So getting a good night's sleep plays a key role in calming the amygdala and decreasing anxiety. Lack of sleep increases reactivity in the amygdala, raising our general levels of anxiety and making us more sensitive to other emotional states such as anger and irritability.

So how much sleep is sufficient? Eight hours of sleep is normally the magic number suggested to ensure the brain is performing at its best, but recent research suggests it varies from individual to individual, and the optimal time is somewhere between seven to nine hours. However, these recommendations miss out on an important understanding of the sleep cycle.

The full sleep cycle lasts around ninety minutes and goes through five stages, with the REM part of the sleep cycle being the last stage:

- Stage 1 – Light sleep in which we drift in and out of sleep and can be awakened easily.

- Stage 2 – Still in light sleep. Heart rate slows and body temperature drops. The body is getting ready for deep sleep.
- Stages 3 & 4 – These are the deep sleep stages. Difficult to wake up. No eye movement or muscle activity. Waking in these stages feels disorientating.
- REM Stage – Breathing becomes more rapid, irregular, and shallow, our eyes jerk rapidly in various directions, limb muscles become temporarily paralysed. Heart rate also increases and blood pressure rises. We dream in this stage and waking during REM sleep often comes with bizarre and illogical thoughts as dreams are recalled.

After completing a full cycle we return to the first stage again and repeat this pattern throughout the night. The first few sleep cycles of the night contain relatively short periods of REM sleep, but long periods of deep sleep. However, as the night progresses, the periods of REM sleep increase in length, while deep sleep decreases. By morning, we spend nearly all of our sleep time in stages 1, 2, and REM.

If we wake up during one of the ninety minute cycles, we start again at the first stage when we go back to sleep, regardless of what stage we woke up in. Then we cycle through the stages until we get to the REM stage again. So two hours of sleep, followed by a period of being awake, and then another five hours sleep isn't necessarily the same as seven hours of continuous sleep. You don't carry on where you left off in the cycle, you have to start again at the beginning. Keep this in mind when you're assessing your quality of sleep.

GETTING TO SLEEP WHEN ANXIOUS
Getting a good night's sleep is often a struggle for people with anxiety because the amygdala is regularly in an aroused state and the sympathetic nervous system is chronically activated. This makes going through the sleep cycles more difficult and is often compounded by worrying thoughts that make it more

difficult to drop off. So the key to sleeping well is to try to ensure you're in as calm a state as possible before going to bed, and also finding a strategy that enables you to fall asleep without too much trouble. You may not always have the time to create a calm environment but it's important to take some time do so if sleeping is a problem for you. Once you're able to sleep consistently well, you will be able to be more flexible with your routine.

Creating a Calm State
Activities that will help you to enter a calmer state before going to bed include:

- A consistent and relaxing routine before bedtime – stick to a consistent bedtime on most nights, at least until you start to begin to sleep well. By repeating a regular pattern, you will condition your body and mind to realise it's time to go to sleep. Begin your routine about 30 to 60 minutes before bedtime and build activities into this time that will reduce stimulation and help you relax; such as reading, having a bath, or listening to music.

- Eliminate as much light as possible – avoid television, computers, tablets and smartphones. Numerous studies suggest blue light in the evening disrupts the brain's natural sleep-wake cycles.[38] If you do go online, use an app or software that eliminates blue light on electronic devices. Many can be found by searching for 'blue light' in both iPhone and Android app stores.

- Create an environment conducive to sleep – make your bedroom as dark as possible and remove all distractions to sleep out of the bedroom (electronic devices, televisions, work items etc.).

- Avoid caffeine, alcohol and spicy foods from early evening onwards – these will stimulate your brain and body.

- Exercise earlier in the day – physical activity will help tire your body and make it more ready for sleep, but try to exercise no later than early evening to avoid over stimulating your body before bedtime. This doesn't have to involve going to the gym or running for miles. A short brisk walk can have an excellent impact.

- Avoid napping during the day – this is especially important if you're not getting a full night of sleep.

- Just before you get into bed do some relaxed breathing or a short meditation. Try the 'Panic Attack Exercise 1: Deep Abdominal Breathing' or the 'Calming the Mind Exercise 1: Mindfulness Meditation'.

Strategies to Fall Asleep

While changing your bedtime routine to maximise the chances of going to bed in a calmer state of mind will definitely help with getting to sleep, people who struggle with anxiety often find as soon as they get into bed and can no longer distract themselves, they start worrying or ruminating. This worrying stimulates the cortex, activates the amygdala, and can make dropping off to sleep very difficult. So what can we do to help us drop off to sleep quickly?

Some of the traditional methods used for getting to sleep, such as counting sheep, are often ineffective. Just knowing we are consciously trying to get to sleep often makes it very difficult, and boredom inducing strategies tend to make our anxious thoughts even more attractive and often keep us awake for longer. However, there are some exercises known to be effective:

1. Cognitive shuffling – This involves mentally picturing a random object for a few seconds before moving onto another: a carton of milk, a car, a castle, a paperclip, and so on. It's important to ensure the sequence is truly meaningless, otherwise you'll drift back into rumination.

This method was developed by Canadian scientist Luc Beaudoin, and described by journalist Oliver Burkeman in his health and wellbeing column in The Guardian newspaper.[39] The exercise is based on the theory the brain tests if it's safe to fall asleep by checking what our cortex is doing. If the cortex is engaged in rational thinking activity, it determines it may be considering dangers and it would therefore be best for us to stay awake. However, if the thoughts are random nonsense, the brain considers we are relaxed and tired, and sleep should be induced.

Cognitive shuffling also reduces rumination by the simple fact that it's difficult to focus your attention on more than one thing at a time. It's hard to ruminate about a problem at work if you're busy generating images of balloons, cheese, and train carriages. Beaudoin has an app that provides random words and speaks them into your ear. However, I'd suggest avoiding using an app or headphones in bed, as sleep aids like this, while useful for a time, can act as a crutch, and make sleeping without them difficult in the future. Instead, it would be more effective create these random words yourself by going through the alphabet and naming as many items as you can think of for each letter before going on to the next.

2. Scanning through your day in detail – This exercise involves mentally going through your day in detail, starting from the moment you woke up. So when you get into bed, close your eyes and recall the very first moment of the day you can remember, and then scan through the day as if you're fast forwarding a video. Don't do this too quickly, just do your best to remember all the different parts of the day. It has a certain rhythm to it. So it might be something like this: I woke up – walked to the bathroom – went to the toilet – brushed my teeth – had a shower – woke my child – went into the kitchen – made the breakfast – brushed my teeth – walked to the car – drove to work, and so on. Just work your way through the day remembering all of the different things you did. It should take a few minutes. You may get to parts of the day you'd like to pause and spend a little bit of time thinking about, but don't pause, just keep going, leave that behind. Let go of the conversation or situation you'd like to focus on and continue to work your way up right up to the present time when you're in bed. Notice when your mind wanders off from scanning the day, and when you realise it's wandered, just gently bring it back to the scanning, starting up again from you left off.

When you've finished scanning through your day, very slowly start to become aware of your breath. Don't change it, but just be aware of it. Count your breaths until you get to ten. If you lose count or your mind wanders, don't worry, just bring your attention back to your breath and start again from one. If you're still awake at this stage, start counting backwards from 100 right the way down to zero, not with the intention of falling asleep but with the intention of getting to zero. If you're still awake after reaching zero, start again at 100 and count down again, and keep repeating this.

3. Sleep meditation – there is an extended audio guide version of the above exercise, with a few extra stages in, including a meditation tailored for sleep. If you find you are still unable to sleep. You can access and download the exercise here: https://soundcloud.com/dr-matt-lewis/sleep-meditation

Physical Activity

I think we all now know physical activity is good for our physical health. There's growing evidence physical activity can lower the risk of a number of ailments and disorders, ranging from type 2 diabetes, to heart disease, to cancer.[40] However, maybe less well known is the gathering evidence illustrating the positive impact of physical exercise on mental wellbeing,[41] and more specifically, anxiety.[42]

PHYSICAL ACTIVITY REDUCES ANXIETY SYMPTOMS

Research has shown physical exercise can measurably reduce anxiety in around twenty minutes, which is less time than it takes most medications to start working.[43] Physical activity is not only effective at reducing the physiological symptoms of anxiety, but has also been demonstrated to calm the amygdala – reducing its reactivity – meaning anxious feelings and their symptoms are less likely to start, or are much reduced.[44] & [45]

This shouldn't really surprise us, as when anxiety triggers the fight, flight, or freeze response, it prepares our body to move quickly and powerfully. Physical activity uses the emergency response in the way it was intended – by moving and being active. Being physically active lowers the levels of adrenaline pumping through the body and uses glucose released into the bloodstream. So exercise calms the amygdala and reduces anxious thoughts and the physical symptoms. Importantly, it also positively impacts on mental health by producing feelings of wellbeing and exhilaration, prompted by the release of neurotransmitters called endorphins, which also work on reducing pain.

However, exercise is not just an antidote to acute anxiety symptoms, it has also been shown to have a long-term effect on anxiety, with evidence it significantly reduces chronic anxiety, working at least as well as medication over long periods.[46] & [47] Regular exercise also has the benefit of providing long lasting muscle relaxation, which, like the muscle relaxation exercises we outlined earlier, reduces muscle tension throughout the body and in turn dampens amygdala reactivity, further contributing to lower levels of anxiety.[48]

PHYSICAL ACTIVITY AS EXPOSURE TREATMENT

Exercise can also be particularly beneficial for people who struggle with panic attacks or the strong physiological symptoms of anxiety or stress. Moderate physical activity can act as a type of exposure treatment, helping us to get used to the physical sensations often experienced when anxious or stressed. Experiencing similar sensations while exercising (increased heart rate, rapid breathing, elevated blood pressure) helps us to realise they are not harmful, but we can cope with them and get used to the discomfort.[49]

BUT I DON'T LIKE PHYSICAL ACTIVITY

I've read and taught about the benefits of physical activity for a long time, but have also noticed, despite growing evidence of the benefits of exercise and exhortations to get more active from the media, health experts, and government campaigns, most people still don't exercise regularly. In order for people to be motivated to exercise they must either enjoy what they are doing, or it has to be a part of normal everyday life, whether it be through necessity or choice. My love of walking came from having to walk 25 minutes to the train station from my home and then another 20 minutes after getting off to the train to my place of work every day. If I'd had my own car at the time, I probably would have driven to the train station. However, four years of enforced walking turned into a habit I love, and I've long continued to walk everyday despite no longer needing to do the same daily commute.

People often find physical activity difficult to start and maintain because it is seen as a chore. Exercise has become synonymous with going to the gym, and while some people love visiting the gym, for many of us, the gym is a sterile, artificial, and intimidating environment that can be off putting. So the most important criteria for deciding on what type of exercise you should do is enjoyment. If we enjoy what we are doing we are more likely to keep on doing it. Think about what exercise you can do outside of the gym, whether it's at a club, at home, or outside.

Exercising outside – in nature – known as 'green exercise', has been shown to have extra mental health benefits above and beyond physical activity. These include improvements in mood and self-esteem, and reductions in anxiety and depression.[50] I may be biased due to my love of walking, but having taught about the benefits of exercise for many years, I am convinced that if there is a panacea in medicine, it's walking. So if you do nothing else, start walking for 10 to 20 minutes a day and slowly introduce more walking into your everyday life. The recommended dose is 10,000 steps a day, which is about 4.5 miles. Get a pedometer or activity monitor, such as a Fitbit, to see how far you're walking. Build up to a level of fitness that allows you to walk briskly for some of the time.

Whatever exercise you do, try to do it with moderate intensity and also make sure your doctor approves it. Think about incorporating it into '*Foundational Exercise 2: Balancing Life*' outlined in the Calming the Mind part of the book.

Assess Your Media Diet

We've talked about our human negativity bias a number of times already. This survival strategy, inherited from our early ancestors, who lived in very dangerous environments, naturally draws our attention to negative news stories. So it's no surprise that negative stories dominate the media and we feel compelled to watch. It's natural to want to follow updates of terrorist events, violence, shootings, and war, both on television and social media.

Anything that alerts us to possible incoming danger, near or far, catches our attention very easily. However, repeated exposure to trauma by the media can have as similar an impact as experiencing the event first-hand.

HOW CONSTANTLY CONSUMING THE NEWS CAN INCREASE ANXIETY

You may think it is necessary to keep up with the news, and those who follow the media closely are more informed about the dangers of the world, but this isn't the case. In fact, people who digest more media, grossly overestimate rates of violence.[51] We can compound this and raise our levels of anxiety and helplessness further by reading fearful and angry public comments on what has happened and what action should be taken. Consuming the news in this way makes us far more anxious and afraid because we don't tend to be very good at assessing risk. We overestimate our chances of being in danger due to a number of irrational ways of thinking. Some of these include:

- If a recent event is particularly dramatic and receives saturation coverage in the media we tend to overestimate the risk of something similar happening to ourselves. We do not see dramatic in-depth media coverage of other causes of death which are more common, such as road traffic accidents, so we assume the events that receive more coverage are more dangerous to us.

- We lack awareness of the more common positive or neutral events. We don't focus on the far more common non-events that occur every day, such as the number of flights that safely arrive at an airport, or the number of positive social interactions between people of different religions. These events, which are a far more accurate indicator of reality, do not make the news as they are common and are more likely to occur.

- We succumb to the recency effect. We think a dramatic event is more likely to happen if a similar event happened recently. This is the case after terrorist attacks, virus outbreaks such as Ebola, and aeroplane accidents.

IS THE WORLD BECOMING LESS SAFE?

Although it sometimes feels like the world is becoming less safe, peaceful and united, and therefore more dangerous, violent, and divided, is this actually the case? If you look at the measurements objectively, the world we currently live in is probably more peaceful, safe, and less dangerous, than at any other time.[52] & [53] Despite this, most of us have never felt as disturbed about the world before, so it feels as if things are worse.

What has changed is how we are getting our information; there are now far more cameras to record both small and large incidents, an internet that helps us to spread information more easily and widely, and also the far reaching effects of social media. So the type of information we now receive has changed, along with the way we get it.

We are living in an attention economy and the information that gets the most attention is extremism and fear mongering. As we've discussed before, our negativity bias naturally gravitates towards this type of information, even if it is unbalanced. So extreme views are rewarded with more attention, more shares, and more comments. Social media, some news channels, and the internet in general, have developed a medium in which moderate views, respectful discussion, and reasonable behaviour is considered boring and uninteresting.

DISTRACTION AND COGNITIVE OVERLOAD

Continual media exposure also distracts us from getting on with other activities we need to do, or would benefit from, and can also overload our thinking. Endless access to new information easily overwhelms our working memory. When we reach cognitive overload, our ability to transfer learning to long-term memory significantly deteriorates. It's as if our brain has become a full cup of water and anything more poured into it starts to spill out. So we leave ourselves with little time to do other things properly and are also unable to focus as well on other information.

You also may have noticed once you start looking at news and social media, it's difficult to stop, it almost becomes an addiction. Our brain craves continual stimulation, is drawn to novelty, and likes to be instantly gratified. Continually watching or reading updates creates a compulsion loop, and like drug addicts, we need more and more 'hits' to get the same effect.

As a personal example, I remember when I used to view social media very frequently. I found sometimes when I closed my eyes at night, went in the shower, or did anything that didn't take up my full attention, my head would be full of the voices of those I followed on social media. They were constantly swirling around my head. I'd be party to arguments between others that didn't concern me, engrossed in problems I could do nothing about, and overloaded with so much information I couldn't process it all.

After a while I realised the thoughts of others were robbing me of any peace or quiet, and were not even allowing my own thoughts to come through. My head was full of well-meaning advice, angry views, outraged voices, stories of injustice, fear, grudges, research findings, funny quips, and many polarised opinions. Meanwhile I realised my life was being lived through the lens of others.

HOW SHOULD WE STAY INFORMED?

This is not to say we should never catch up on the news or engage in social media, or that it always has a negative effect. The internet and social media has also been a vehicle for good and provides some people with a voice and positive connections they previously didn't have access to. However, we should raise our awareness of how often we access certain types of media and reflect on how we feel after this exposure. We should consider what types of news we digest and what sources we rely on.

Plan times when you want to catch up with the news rather than accessing it continually, and try to notice when you're automatically checking for updates without being aware of what you're doing. If, after reflection, you become aware your media diet is problematic and adds to your anxiety, consider how you might change the way you consume the news and any other media, and incorporate it into 'Foundational Exercise 2: Balancing Life.'

Looking Outwards:
Focusing Away from You and Your Anxiety

When we're looking to overcome our anxiety, we often focus intensely on ourselves as we try to find a solution. This is understandable, as anxiety is an individual state. When feeling very anxious it seems reasonable to think we should focus our attention inwards in order to 'work' on ourselves and assess how effective the strategies and exercises are in helping us.

However, while some self-evaluation is necessary – we do need to know what's working after all – intense self-focus has also been shown to be harmful to wellbeing. A wealth of evidence has demonstrated anxiety already tends to turn people inwards. It makes us more introspective and therefore less socially engaged and lonelier, and this self-focus can also undermine happiness and cause depression.[54] It's like a vicious circle; we feel anxious, so we withdraw and become introspective, but this in turn makes us more anxious.

Alongside this, to find out if we're making progress, we often compare our past levels of anxiety to our current levels of anxiety. This creates a problem: the moment we make that comparison, we shift from experiencing life to evaluating life.

Consider the research on a concept called flow – a state of complete absorption in an activity. Researchers have found when people are in a flow state, they don't report on any particular emotion – being happy, sad, anxious, fearful – as they're too busy concentrating on the activity. But afterwards, looking back, they describe flow as a positive emotion. If we become busy assessing each new strategy and evaluation, we can never fully engage in activities, projects, relationships and life in general. Instead, we can become anxious and depressed and enter a vicious circle. This is documented by psychologists Katariina Salmela-Aro and Jari-Erik Nurmi: anxiety and depression leads people to evaluate their daily projects as less enjoyable, and ruminating about why they're not fun makes the anxiety and depression worse.[55]

So what can we learn from this research? Firstly, we should start engaging with exercises and projects without constantly evaluating how anxious we are, and focus instead on the exercises or projects themselves. Some reflection on whether the exercises are effective, and which ones work best, can be valuable, but we should avoid constantly evaluating our anxiety and happiness. Secondly, we should be wary of becoming too self-focused or self-absorbed with ourselves and our anxiety, and attempt to also look outwards towards other people.

Some interesting research from the University of British Columbia discovered that encouraging people who suffer from anxiety to engage with others, through acts of kindness, helped reduce anxiety.[56] The researchers recruited participants who reported experiencing high levels of social anxiety, and randomly assigned them to three groups for a four-week intervention. One group performed acts of kindness, another group was simply exposed to social interactions, and the last group was given no instructions except to record what happened each day. The results found those individuals who were asked to perform acts of kindness had the greatest overall decrease in their anxiety about social interactions. That is, they were less scared of, and more drawn to, socialising with others.

The theory behind the results is that by trying to protect themselves from being evaluated negatively by other people, anxious people don't socially interact. This in turn means any chance to demonstrate their perceptions may be wrong are cut off. The acts of kindness helped to counter this fear of negative evaluation as the anxious people found people responded more positively to them than they expected.

So in the midst of practising all of the exercises we've outlined, don't constantly withdraw into your own world, but also look to how you can help and interact with others.

*

Finally

You did it, you made it to the very end! Thank you for taking the time to read all the way through, I hope this book has equipped you to understand your anxiety more fully and given you the tools to overcome it and move forward in life. It has been a labour of love for me, and I've found I've regularly had to use the skills I've written about to finish the task. The only final request I have is that you start to practically apply the exercises. Nothing will change if you only read the book. You must take action.

I wish you all health, happiness and a life of courage.

Matthew Lewis, Newcastle upon Tyne, 2016.

Further Details and Resources

Contact Details

If you have any feedback, suggestions, or questions, please feel free to contact me at Matt@DrMattLewis.com or by tweeting me @mattlewis

If you have enjoyed this book I would be very grateful if you would leave a review on Amazon.

Meditations

All meditations can be found at:
https://soundcloud.com/dr-matt-lewis

Power Poses

Illustrations of power poses can be found at:
http://www.drmattlewis.com/power-poses/

Online Course

The original online course can been found at a discounted price here: Udemy Discount
www.udemy.com/overcome-anxiety/?couponCode=BOOK01

ABOUT THE AUTHOR

Dr Matt Lewis holds a Ph.D. in psychology and is a former university academic who now delivers public and online courses in emotional wellbeing and personal development. He lectured in health psychology, exercise psychology, and mental health to undergraduate and postgraduate students, while also designing and delivering courses in mindfulness, positive psychology, and Acceptance and Commitment Training (ACT) to the general public, trainers, teachers, and health professionals.

Notes

1. McGonigal, K. (2015). The Upside of Stress: Why Stress is Good for You (and How to Get Good at It). Vermilion, London, U.K.

2. Crum, A.J. and Langer, E.J. (2007). Mind-set matters: exercise and the placebo effect. *Psychological Science*, 18 (2), pp. 165-171.

3. Crum, A.J., Corbin, W.R., Brownell, K.D. and Salovey, P. (2011). Mind over milkshakes: mindsets, not just nutrients, determine ghrelin response. *Health Psychology*, 30 (4), pp. 424-129.

4. Crum, A.J., Akinola, M., Martin, A. and Fath, S. (In Progress). Improving stress without reducing stress: the benefits of a stress enhancing mindset in both challenging and threatening contexts. In: McGonigal, K. (2015). The Upside of Stress: Why Stress is Good for You (and How to Get Good at It). Vermilion, London, U.K., pp. 7-10.

5. Boudarene, M., Legros, J.J. and Timsit-Berthier, (2001). Study of the stress response: role of anxiety, cortisol, and DHEAs. *L'Encephale*, 28 (2), pp. 139-146.

6. McGonigal, K. (2015). The Upside of Stress: Why Stress is Good for You (and How to Get Good at It). Vermilion, London, U.K., pp. 28-32

7. Cocking, C. (2016). Brussels terror attack victims show how humans help each other in times of crisis. [ONLINE] Available at: https://theconversation.com/brussels-terror-attack-victims-show-how-humans-help-each-other-in-times-of-crisis-56707. [Accessed 17 June 2016].

8. Syed, M. (2015). Black Box Thinking: The Surprising Truth About Success (and Why Some People Never Learn from Their Mistakes). John Murray, London, U.K., pp. 135-141.

9. Ito, T.A., Larsen, J.T., Smith, N.K. and Cacioppo, J.T. (1998). Negative Information Weighs More Heavily on the Brain: The Negativity Bias in Evaluative Categorizations. *Journal of Personality and Social Psychology*, 75 (4), pp. 887-900.

10. McLeod, S. A. (2010). Stress, Illness and the Immune System. Retrieved from www.simplypsychology.org/stress-immune.html

11. Draganski, B., Gaser, C., Busch, V., Schuierer, G., Bogdahn, U. and May, A. (2005). Neuroplasticity: Changes in grey matter induced by training. *NeuroReport*, 16 (17), pp. 1893–1897.

12. Pittman, C.M. and Karle, E.M. (2015). Rewire Your Anxious Brain: How to Use the Neuroscience of Fear to End Anxiety, Panic and Worry. New Harbinger Publications, Oakland, pp. 38.

13. Harris, R. (2008). The Happiness Trap. Robinson, London, U.K.

14. Boyd, T.L. and Levis, D.J. (1983). Exposure is a necessary condition for fear-reduction: A reply to De Silva and Rachman. *Behaviour Research and Therapy*, 21 (2), pp. 143-149.

15. Dickerson, S.S. and Kemeny, M.E. (2004). Acute stressors and cortisol responses: a theoretical integration and synthesis of laboratory research. *Psychological Bulletin*, 130, 355-391.

16. Pip, S. (2015). Jon Ronson Part 1. Distraction Pieces Podcast with Scroobius Pip. N.p., 2015. Web. 22 June 2016.

17. Williams, M. and Penman, D. (2011). Mindfulness: A Practical Guide to Finding Peace in a Frantic World. Hachette, London, U.K., pp. 211-216.

18. Dijksterhuis, A.P., Bos, M.W., Nordgren, L.F. and van Baaren, R.B. (2006). On making the right choice: The deliberation-without-attention effect. In: Newport, C. (2016). Deep Work: Rules for Focused Success in a Distracted World. Piatkus, London, U.K., pp. 144-145.

19. Berman, M.G., Jonides, J. and Kaplan, S. (2008). The cognitive benefits of interacting with nature. *Psychological Science*, 19 (12), pp. 1207-1212.

20. Berman, M.G. (2012). Berman on the Brain: How to Boost Your Focus. [ONLINE] Available at: http://www.huffingtonpost.ca/marc-berman/attention-restoration-theory-nature_b_1242261.html [Accessed 20 June 2016].

21. Newport, C. (2016). Deep Work: Rules for Focused Success in a Distracted World. Piatkus, London, U.K., pp. 149-150.

22. Rizzolatti, G. and Craighero, L. (2004). The mirror-neuron system. *Annual Review of Neuroscience*, 27 (1), pp. 169-192.

23. Gerber, P., Schlaffke, L., Heba, S., Greenlee, M.W., Schultz T. and Schmidt-Wilcke T. (2014). Juggling revisited - a voxel-based morphometry study with expert jugglers. *Neuroimage*, 15 (95), pp. 320-325.

24a. Treadway, M.T. and Lazar, S. (2008). The Neurobiology of Mindfulness. In Germer,C.K., Siegel, R.D. and Fulton, P.R. (2013). Mindfulness and Psychotherapy. 2nd ed. New York: Guilford Press, pp. 183

24b. Gard,T., Hölzel, B.K. and Lazar, S.W. (2014). The potential effects of meditation on age-related cognitive decline: a systematic review. *Annals of the New York Academy of Sciences*, 1307, pp. 89–103. http://doi.org/10.1111/nyas.12348

25. Davidson, R.J. and Begley, S. (2012). The Emotional Life of your Brain: How Its Unique Patterns Affect the Way You Think, Feel, and Live – and How You Can Change Them. Hudson Street Press, New York, N.Y.

26. Jerath, R., Barnes, V.A., Dillard-Wright, D., Jerath, S. and Hamilton, B. (2012). Dynamic change of awareness during meditation techniques: neural and physiological correlates. *Frontiers in Human Science*, pp. 6, 1-4.

27. Lazar, S.W., Kerr, C.E., Wasserman, R.H., Gray, J.R., Greve, D.N., Treadway, M.T., McGarvey M., Quinn B.T., Dusek J.A., Benson H., Rauch S.L., Moore C.I. and Fischl, B. (2005). Meditation Experience Is Associated with Increased Cortical Thickness. *NeuroReport*, 16 (17), pp. 1893–1897.

28. Cuddy, A.J.C., Wilmuth, C.A., Yap, A J. and Carney, D.R. (2015). Preparatory power posing affects nonverbal presence and job interview performance. *Journal of Applied Psychology*, 100 (4), pp. 1286-1295.

29. Brooks, A. W. (2014). Get excited: Reappraising pre-performance anxiety as excitement. Journal of Experimental Psychology: General, 143, pp. 1144– 1158.

30. Harris, R. (2011). The Confidence Gap. Robinson, U.K., pp. 31-33

31. Campbell, A. (2015). Winners and How They Succeed. Penguin Random House, U.K., pp. 206-207.

32. Campbell, A. (2015). Winners and How They Succeed. Penguin Random House, U.K., pp. 203-204.

33. Campbell, A. (2015). Winners and How They Succeed. Penguin Random House, U.K., pp. 204-205.

34. Ferriss, T. (2015). Tara Brach On Overcoming Challenges And The Fear Of Missing Out. The Tim Ferriss Podcast. N.p., 2015. Web. 7 June 2016.

35. LeDoux, J. E., and J. M. Gorman. (2001). A Call to Action: Overcoming Anxiety Through Active Coping. *American Journal of Psychiatry*, 158, pp. 1953–1955.

36. Kouider, S., Andrillon, T., Barbosa, L.S., Goupil, L. and Bekinschtein, T.A. (2014). *Current Biology*, 24 (18), pp. 2208-2214.

37. Van der Helm, E., Yao, J., Dutt, S., Rao, V., Saletin, J. M., and Walker, M. P. (2011). REM Sleep Depotentiates Amygdala Activity to Previous Emotional Experiences. *Current Biology* : CB, 21(23), 2029–2032.
http://doi.org/10.1016/j.cub.2011.10.052

38. Changa, A.M., Aeschbacha, D., Duffy J.F., and Czeislera, C.A. (2014). Evening use of light-emitting eReaders negatively affects sleep, circadian timing, and next-morning alertness. *Proceedings of the National Academy of Sciences*, 112(4). DOI: 10.1073/pnas.1418490112

39. Burkeman, O. (2016). Shuffle your thoughts and sleep. [ONLINE] Available at:
https://www.theguardian.com/lifeandstyle/2016/jul/15/shuffle-thoughts-sleep-oliver-burkeman. [Accessed 29 July 2016].

40. Lee, I., et al. (2012). Effect of physical inactivity on major non-communicable diseases worldwide: an analysis of burden of disease and life expectancy. *Lancet*, 380, pp. 219-229.

41. Ratey, J.J. (2010). Spark!: The Revolutionary New Science of Exercise and the Brain. Quercus, London.

42. DeBoer, L. B., Powers, M. B., Utschig, A. C., Otto, M. W. and Smits, J. A. (2012). Exploring exercise as an avenue for the treatment of anxiety disorders. *Expert Review of Neurotherapeutics*, 12(8), pp. 1011–1022. http://doi.org/10.1586/ern.12.73

43. Johnsgard, K. W. (2004). Conquering Depression and Anxiety Through Exercise. Prometheus Books, Amherst, NY.

44. Broocks A., Meyer, T., Gleiter, C.H., Hillmer-Vogel, U., George, A., Bartmann, U. and Bandelow B. (2001). Effect of aerobic exercise on behavioral and neuroendocrine responses to meta-chlorophenylpiperazine and to ipsapirone in untrained healthy subjects. *Psychopharmacology*, 155 (3), pp. 234-241.

45. Heisler, L.K., Zhou, L., Bajwa, P., Hsu, J. and Tecott L.H. (2007). Serotonin 5-HT(2C) receptors regulate anxiety-like behavior. *Genes Brain Behavior*, 6 (5), pp. 491-496.

46. Biddle, S.J.H., Mutrie, N. and Gorely, T. (2015). Psychology of Physical Activity: Determinants, Well-Being and Interventions. Routledge, U.K., pp. 96-119.

47. Ratey, J.J. (2010). Spark!: The Revolutionary New Science of Exercise and the Brain. Quercus, London, pp. 85-112.

48. Broman-Fulks, J.J. and Storey, K.M. (2008). Evaluation of a brief aerobic exercise intervention for high anxiety sensitivity. *Anxiety, Stress & Coping*, 21 (2), pp. 117-128.

49. Williams, S.E., Carroll, D., Veldhuijzen van Zanten, J.J.C.S. and Ginty, A.T. (2016). Anxiety symptom interpretation: A potential mechanism explaining the cardiorespiratory fitness–anxiety relationship. *Journal of Affective Disorders*, 193, pp. 151-156.

50. Barton, J., Bragg, R., Wood, C. and Pretty, J. (2016). Green Exercise: Linking Nature, Health and Well-being. Routledge: U.K.

51. Gerbner, G., Gross, L. Morgan, M. and Signorielli. N. (1980). The "Mainstreaming" of America: Violence Profile No. 11. *Journal of Communication*. 30 (3), pp. 10-29.

52. Pinker, S. (2012). The Better Angels of Our Nature: A History of Violence and Humanity. Penguin: London, U.K.

53. The Fallen. Retrieved from http://www.fallen.io/ww2/

54. Mauss, I.B., Savino, N.S., Anderson, C.L., Weisbuch, M., Tamir, M. and Laudenslager, M.L. (2012). The pursuit of happiness can be lonely. *Emotion*, 12(5), pp. 908-912.

55. Salmela-Aro, K. and Nurmi J.K. (1996). Depressive symptoms and personal project appraisals: A cross-lagged longitudinal study. *Personality and Individual Differences*, 21 (3), PP. 373-381.

56. Trew, J.L. and Alden, L.E. (2015). Kindness reduces avoidance goals in socially anxious individuals. *Motivation and Emotion*, 39(6), PP. 892-907.

57. Mayer, V. (2016). Perfect Proofreading: Spot Mistakes Others Miss. Shiborah: Southampton, UK.

84170475R00106

Made in the USA
San Bernardino, CA
04 August 2018